Making Money From
STOCKS & SHARES

Visit our How To website at **www.howto.co.uk**

At **www.howto.co.uk** you can engage in conversation with our authors – all of whom have 'been there and done that' in their specialist fields. You can get access to special offers and additional content but most importantly you will be able to engage with, and become a part of, a wide and growing community of people just like yourself.

At **www.howto.co.uk** you'll be able to talk and share tips with people who have similar interests and are facing similar challenges in their lives. People who, just like you, have the desire to change their lives for the better – be it through moving to a new country, starting a new business, growing their own vegetables, or writing a novel.

At **www.howto.co.uk** you'll find the support and encouragement you need to help make your aspirations a reality.

You can do direct to **www.making-money-from-stocks-and-shares.co.uk** which is part of the main How To site.

How To Books strives to present authentic, inspiring, practical information in their books. Now, when you buy a title from **How To Books**, you get even more than just words on a page.

Making Money From
STOCKS & SHARES

A simple guide to increasing your wealth
by consistent investment in the stock market

Jamie E Smith

howtobooks

Published by How To Books
Spring Hill House, Spring Hill Road
Begbroke, Oxford OX5 1RX, United Kingdom
Tel: (01865) 375794 Fax: (01865) 379162
info@howtobooks.co.uk
www.howtobooks.co.uk

How To Books greatly reduce the carbon footpring of their books by sourcing
their typesetting and printing in the UK.

British Library Cataloguing in Publication Data
A catalogue record for this book is available from the British Library

ISBN 978 1 84528 431 2

Produced for How To Books by Deer Park Productions, Tavistock
Typeset by Kestrel Data, Exeter
Printed and bound in Great Britain by Bell & Bain Ltd, Glasgow

NOTE: The material contained in this book is set out in good faith for general
guidance and no liability can be accepted for loss or expense incurred as a
result of relying in particular circumstances on statements made in the book.
The laws and regulations are complex and liable to change, and readers should
check the current position with the relevant authorities before making
personal arrangements.

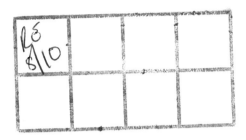

For Caroline, Charlotte and Alexander

'Whether you think you can or whether you think you can't, you're right.'

Henry Ford – Founder of the Ford Motor Company

&

**Dedicated to the memory of Elizabeth Smith
1948–2009**

Contents

About the author

Jamie E. Smith is a business graduate with an MBA, currently working with the executive team of a large public sector organisation in the field of strategic planning. He has over a decade's worth of experience of investing in the stock market and increasing (not quite Warren Buffet, but at least he practises what he is writing about). He has travelled from eastern China to western California and back again, and settled in the village of Great Haywood in Stafford, England, where he lives with his wife, two kids, two cats (Phil and Pog), two horses, two fish and countless fleas.

The author currently holds an interest in the following companies, amongst others:

Coca Cola, Alliance Trust, Vodafone, Rolls Royce, Tesco, Henderson Far East Income Ltd, Wells Fargo, Hansard Global, National Grid, Barclays, BP, GlaxoSmithKline, Ladbrokes, Aberdeen New Dawn Investment Trust, Harley Davidson, William Hill, Thorntons, City of London Investment Group, Bunzl, BAE Systems, Provident Financial, Royal Dutch Shell, QinetiQ, H & T Group and Aberdeen Asian Income Fund.

Desiderata

Go placidly amid the noise and the haste,
and remember what peace there may be in silence.
As far as possible, without surrender,
be on good terms with all persons.
Speak your truth quietly and clearly;
and listen to others,
even to the dull and the ignorant;
they too have their story.

Avoid loud and aggressive persons;
they are vexatious to the spirit.
If you compare yourself with others,
you may become vain or bitter,
for always there will be greater and lesser persons than yourself.
Enjoy your achievements as well as your plans.
Keep interested in your own career, however humble;
it is a real possession in the changing fortunes of time.
Exercise caution in your business affairs,
for the world is full of trickery.
But let this not blind you to what virtue there is;
many persons strive for high ideals,
and everywhere life is full of heroism.

Be yourself. Especially do not feign affection.
Neither be cynical about love,
for in the face of all aridity and disenchantment,
it is as perennial as the grass.
Take kindly the counsel of the years,
gracefully surrendering the things of youth.
Nurture strength of spirit to shield you in sudden misfortune.
But do not distress yourself with dark imaginings.
Many fears are born of fatigue and loneliness.

Beyond a wholesome discipline,
be gentle with yourself.
You are a child of the universe
no less than the trees and the stars;
you have a right to be here.
And whether or not it is clear to you,
no doubt the universe is unfolding as it should.
Therefore, be at peace with God,
whatever you conceive Him to be.
And whatever your labors and aspirations,
in the noisy confusion of life,
keep peace in your soul.

With all its sham, drudgery, and broken dreams,
it is still a beautiful world.
Be cheerful. Strive to be happy.

Max Ehrmann

CHAPTER 1:

Introduction

A MISER sold all that he had and bought a lump of gold, which he buried in a hole in the ground by the side of an old wall and went to look at daily.

One of his workmen observed his frequent visits to the spot and decided to watch his movements. He soon discovered the secret of the hidden treasure, and digging down, came to the lump of gold, and stole it.

The Miser, on his next visit, found the hole empty and began to tear his hair and to make loud lamentations.

A neighbour, seeing him overcome with grief and learning the cause, said, 'Pray do not grieve so; but go and take a stone, and place it in the hole, and fancy that the gold is still lying there. It will do you quite the same service; for when the gold was there, you had it not, as you did not make the slightest use of it.'

Aesop

I have always been interested in business. Although I didn't realise it when I was younger, I have always wanted to work on something that grows. Growing things is a creative process, and whether you are a gardener, an investor, or a parent, growing things is one of the most rewarding of human endeavours. When I discovered the stock market and realised just how potentially easy it was to buy shares and in theory watch your money grow, I was hooked. Of course, buying shares worth buying was the challenge and whilst a learning curve undoubtedly exists, it is one that is perhaps not as steep or as challenging as is widely believed.

This book will introduce you to some principles of and take you through some approaches to investing in stocks and shares, and will show you how it may not be half as complicated as you first thought.

INVESTING IS BETTER THAN SAVING

Most wealthy people have known for a long time how to accrue wealth and the money that can be made from investing wisely. Some pay others to do this for them and there is no shortage of money managers to choose from who can provide such a service. However, for most people, this may not be a viable option and you may find yourself left with limited choice and scope for your money. Most of the people I know put their savings into the best ISA they can find, thinking it to be a wise investment. It may be a low-risk investment or way of saving, but even in times of relatively-high interest rates, the returns on most basic savings accounts are unlikely to make you rich.

Although interest rates change over time so your ISA may pay you more or less in the future, they are unlikely to provide the same kind of return that wise investing in the stock market can provide. It has always seemed a great tragedy to me that most ordinary people (by which I mean the kind of person who does not consider themselves to be especially wealthy already) do not take advantage of buying shares in great companies and of all of the benefits that it can provide. It takes only the desire to learn, and some time to familiarise yourself with the initial basic concepts of buying shares, to start to make a difference to your financial health.

LEARN FINANCIAL DIY

You don't need to rely on any expert; in fact, I am not sure where investing is concerned if such a beast even exists. You don't need to have lots of money to start with to make money buying shares, and finally with regard to risk, that is largely a matter of perception. I would imagine that many of the savers in Northern Rock up to 2007 would have considered their accounts to be a safe bet and very low risk. How wrong could they be! We get into our cars each day and take a calculated risk. Drive too fast on unfamiliar roads and sooner or later you are likely to pay a price for your risky behaviour. Abide by some basic and widely-known rules when driving (which everyone knows when they pass their test), research your journey and drive sensibly, and you are less likely to have something unpleasant happen and more likely to achieve your objective. Investing is like that. Everyone knows the rules, but just like drivers, few abide by the good ones. It is not in our nature to do so, but the good news is that we can adapt and learn new skills and accrue new knowledge, and if we take some simple steps in these areas, we can all become our own investing experts.

YOU DON'T NEED TO BE A BUSINESS STUDENT TO BENEFIT FROM THIS BOOK

For the purpose of this book I have deliberately omitted large quantities of technical analysis or anything that could be regarded as comprehensive in any way. That is not because it was easier for me to do this; it is merely something I am happy to leave to the academic world which has already done it in large quantities, and I have nothing to add to that here. This book provides an easy, accessible read that you don't need an academic background to understand.

This book is also aimed at the person who may be open to considering buying shares for the first time, but lacks confidence in how to approach it. Therefore this work explores some simple basic steps that could be taken in approaching this process, hopefully without being patronising in any way.

BE AWARE OF WHAT THIS BOOK IS *NOT* ABOUT

It should also be noted that this book is focused only on buying shares as an investment option, something which I am very well aware is a little like a doctor who knows only about septic fingers. There are, of course, many ways to save and invest and increase your wealth over time. I just happen to have achieved it through buying shares and that remains my personal vehicle of choice, but it would be irresponsible of me not to at least point out that buying shares is not for everyone. If in doubt, do some research and if still in doubt, seek advice from someone appropriately qualified to direct you.

I am hoping that you have already formulated a conclusion about what suits you, and an assumption is made that as you are reading this, you have decided that investing in the stock market is an option that interests you. As such, read on. If you want general financial advice, go and see a financial adviser; and if you are not paying for that advice, bear in mind that someone else probably is.

LET'S TALK ABOUT YOU

Success with investing is as much about your personality and who you are, as it is about being able to understand the financial details of a business. It really is.

Are you the type of person to get carried along with the crowd or succumb to peer pressure? There is nothing to be ashamed of in answering 'Yes' to this question; in fact, if you did, you probably know yourself better than most and you already have an advantage that you probably were not aware of. The majority of people would have answered 'No', and yet we can all see how a majority of people behave in that very way in daily life. Remember that 80% of people allegedly consider themselves to be above average. Being honest with yourself is a critical success factor. More of that later.

In taking a simplistic approach it is inevitable that there will be many omissions and many arguable points. I am solely guilty of any points of contention, and any prejudices about what is worth considering and what is not, are all mine and mine alone. The whole point of this book is to act as a series of signposts. You should be wary of anyone, or any book, that appears to offer strategies, quick solutions or techniques for making money out of the stock market. They are unlikely to be of any use to you. Remember the following as it will serve you well, and we shall explore this point and what it means on several occasions throughout this book:

> **'Lust and greed are more gullible than innocence.'**
>
> Mason Cooley – American aphorist

Right from the start I want to acknowledge a debt of gratitude to some of the world's finest investors from whom I continue to watch and learn. As you read this book there are numerous quotes from some of the world's finest investors, and it is hard to overstate the contribution of such investment masters to the craft of investing, whether it be Benjamin Graham or Warren Buffet or similar. I will refer to the wisdom of such people frequently throughout and make no apology for it. Figures like Warren Buffet are a little like Yoda from *Star Wars*: small in stature and somewhat unassuming but in terms of ability, quite the master.

IF YOU DON'T HAVE TOO MUCH MONEY, READ ON

Making rich people richer does not really motivate me. Increasing the wealth of people who do not consider themselves to be wealthy, and assisting them to achieve their financial goals and grow their wealth is a big motivation in writing this book.

Armed with a basic toolkit of measures from which to adapt a consistent approach to your own personal style, you can begin.

Like many of the finest things in life, such as a work of fine art or a great novel, the stock market works on many levels and can be a rewarding experience for the both the novice and master alike.

> **'If you're poor, change and you'll succeed.'**
>
> Chinese proverb

'Money is better than poverty,
if only for financial reasons.'

Woody Allen – American film director/comedian

Thanks for taking the time to read this book. I hope it will be a worthwhile investment. I also hope that it may start you on a journey that you may otherwise not have taken, and that you continue along that road with an open mind. I wish you every success in the constant learning process that is consistent investing in the stock market, and I hope that you make money doing so.

Please note: neither the publisher or the author are making specific investment recommendations in this book. The case studies and examples are included only to illustrate general investment principles and practice.

CHAPTER 2:

Who do you think you are?

THINK ABOUT HOW YOU BEHAVE

How well do you really know yourself? This is an important question and the starting point for any investor. Understanding your true character and nature, as opposed to the character you would like to think you are, is a critical success factor for the consistent investor. I cannot emphasise enough how important this process is and how important it is to take time to do this properly before you start investing. Do it

'Know thyself'

Socrates – Greek philosopher

properly and it will save you a potentially painful financial experience and what is more, it will equip with you an advantage in your investing career from the very start.

Learning from the tale of the frog and the scorpion

The Scorpion and the Frog

One day, a scorpion looked around at the mountain where he lived and decided that he wanted a change. So he set out on a journey through the forests and hills. He climbed over rocks and under vines and kept going until he reached a river.

The river was wide and swift, and the scorpion stopped to consider the situation. He couldn't see any way across. So he ran upriver and then checked downriver, all the while thinking that he might have to turn back.

Suddenly, he saw a frog sitting in the rushes by the bank on the other side of the river. He decided to ask the frog for help getting across the stream.

'Hellooo, Mr Frog!' called the scorpion across the water. 'Would you be so kind as to give me a ride on your back across the river?'

'Well now, Mr Scorpion! How do I know that if I try to help you, you won't try to kill me?' asked the frog hesitantly.

'Because,' the scorpion replied, 'if I try to kill you, then I would die too, for you see I cannot swim.'

Now this seemed to make sense to the frog. But he asked, 'What about when I get close to the bank? You could still try to kill me and get back to the shore.'

'This is true,' agreed the scorpion, 'but then I wouldn't be able to get to the other side of the river.'

'Alright then . . . how do I know you won't just wait till we get to the other side and THEN kill me?' said the frog.

'Ahh . . .' crooned the scorpion, 'because you see, once you've taken me to the other side of this river, I will be so grateful for your help, that it would hardly be fair to reward you with death, now would it?'

So the frog agreed to take the scorpion across the river. He swam over to the bank and settled himself near the mud to pick up his passenger. The scorpion crawled onto the frog's back, his sharp claws prickling into the frog's soft hide, and the frog slid into the river. The muddy water swirled around them, but the frog stayed near the surface so the scorpion would not drown. He kicked strongly through the first half of the river, his flippers paddling wildly against the current.

Halfway across the river, the frog suddenly felt a sharp sting in his back and, out of the corner of his eye, saw the scorpion remove his stinger from the frog's back. A deadening numbness began to creep into his limbs.

'You fool!' croaked the frog. 'Now we shall both die! Why on earth did you do that?'

The scorpion shrugged, and did a little jig on the drowning frog's back.

'I could not help myself. It is my nature,' said the scorpion.

Unknown author

LEARNING TO CONTROL YOUR BEHAVIOUR

So what can we learn, as investors, from the tale of the frog and the scorpion? It is all about our nature and how we behave under certain circumstances. Some of our basic human behaviours can be very bad for our investing. However, if we are aware of them, we can do something to try and control them and in so doing improve our chances for staying the course and achieving our objectives. This process is about training yourself to both think and more importantly *behave* differently.

The scorpion would have done a lot better to have controlled his nature, at least until he got to the other side. The frog would have done better to trust his own judgement and to stay away from scorpions, full stop. Neither was able to control their behaviours and actions enough not to deviate from what seemed like an obvious set of rules. In truth, we are all a bit like the frog *and* the scorpion, but the trick is not to be too much of either.

'Real knowledge is to know the extent of one's ignorance.'

Confucius – philosopher

AN EXAMPLE TO ILLUSTRATE THE POINT

If you win a small amount of money on the lottery, you are probably more likely to want to buy a ticket the following week even though you are no more likely to win that week than you were the week before you won. Equally, recent events, especially bad ones, are more likely to impact on your decision-making behaviours than events further away. This is why in 2009 few investors were buying banking shares. Equally, when you have just lost something, it is more probable you will see the loss as likely to happen again. A classic example of what I am getting at is when people rush out and buy expensive home security equipment the week *after* they have been burgled. This is because recent negative events have a significant emotional impact that can cause an irrational response. We can easily attach too much significance to a recent negative experience just as we can to a recent positive one. The most successful bookmakers like Ladbrokes and William Hill understand this aspect of human psychology very well. It is not in the interest of such businesses for their customers to lose too often.

> '*Anything you lose automatically doubles in value.*'
>
> Mignon McLaughlin, *The Second Neurotic's Notebook*, 1966

THE STOCK MARKET IS LIKE JEKYLL AND HYDE

The British economist John Maynard Keynes once said:

> '*There is nothing so disastrous as a rational investment policy in an irrational world.*'

Of course, an irrational investment policy in an irrational world would be even more likely to lead to financial disaster.

KEEP YOUR HEAD AND LET OTHERS LOSE THEIRS

What is useful here is an understanding of the irrational nature of the investment world, or to put it another way, people. The stock market very often reflects more about human nature and our irrational behaviours than it does about rational business analysis (*that is not to say that it never gets it right; it does and in many cases a share price tanks for a very good reason*). The rule here is to develop the key analytical and behavioural skills that are necessary to differentiate between when the market is behaving rationally and when it is behaving irrationally. The reason we want to do this is because it is in these circumstances when you are most likely to find a great company whose shares may be selling for a bargain price. Recognising the signs of irrational behaviour is a valuable skill and one that can pay off.

Part of the solution to successful long-term investing is to marry the rational part of your brain with your gut instinct and not irrational behaviours going on around you. Of course in practice this is akin to marrying a cat with a dog. The prize however is worth the effort.

AN ILLUSTRATION OF RATIONAL AND IRRATIONAL BEHAVIOUR

Take the following recent example (Figure 1) of the broad movements in the price of Barclays shares over a ten-year period as an illustration of this point.

Barclays PLC

I have owned Barclays shares for a number of years and have been a keen observer of the bank. Between 2004 and 2007 they increased in value to be trading at £7 a share at various points. They then proceeded to head south between 2007 and the early stages of 2009 when, at one point, they were briefly trading at a little over 50p a share. That is quite a dramatic change and shows just how volatile the stock market can be.

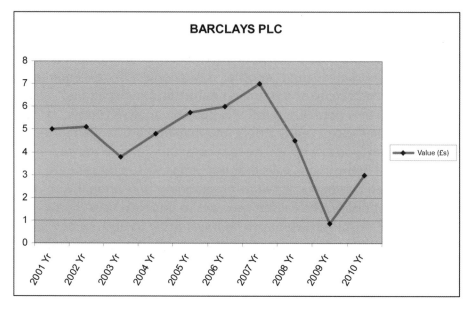

Fig. 1 Price of Barclays shares over ten-year period

'Life is not about waiting for the storm to pass; it is about learning to dance in the rain'.

Unknown

So what did I do in the period between 2004 and 2009? Until well into 2008 I held onto my shares until the world was heading into what was clearly a serious financial mess and a recession that was showing many similarities to the 1930s. I sold a large portion, but not all, of my Barclays shares for a little over £3 in 2008 and I sat and watched. I did not sell these shares because I was in a panic. It was a calculated, rational and well-considered move.

A RATIONAL RESPONSE TO AN IRRATIONAL WORLD

The price of Barclays shares continued to slide, and nobody knew for certain what was going to happen. Once the shares had dropped to around the 60p mark, despite the fact that the world's press and most 'investors' were jumping ship from anything vaguely related to banking shares, and in many cases any shares at all, I started buying back into Barclays in what to me were large quantities. I could do this without spending any real additional money because I had sold my Barclays shares for more than £3 and I could now buy them back for around 60p. At the time, this required a steady nerve and trust in myself that I knew what I was doing despite everyone else considering this to be a sure way to lose all of my money. After all, at that time it looked as though any bank could end up completely nationalised. I thought otherwise and maintained my faith in my approach.

So what does this mean? Well let's say for simplicity, I had 1,000 shares I sold for £3 each: I would then have had £3,000 in cash. Let's say I then bought £3,000 worth of Barclays shares at 60p each. That would give me 5,000 shares in Barclays worth £3,000. What happened next was unusual and not entirely what I would have expected.

RATIONAL MAY BE BORING, BUT YOU GET RICH THAT WAY

I bought back into Barclays because I felt that the market, by which I mean people, were behaving irrationally and had undervalued the bank. The world was caught up in a media frenzy which for the wise can be a world of opportunity. It was my view at that time that Barclays was a relatively-sound business that had found itself in a storm and, whilst having some exposure to bad debts which may rise, it was a diversified enough business with a strong enough management team for the risk-to-reward ratio to be in my favour at the 60p price.

Several months later, the share price of Barclays had reached the £3.50 mark. If we were to apply this to the previous figure we can calculate the investment to be worth £17,500. A satisfactory return on the £3,000 invested.

'We are more often treacherous through weakness than through calculation.'

Francois de la Rochefoucauld – French author, 1630–1680

It is not about buying and selling. It is about knowing when you need to sell, and when you need to buy, and when you need to do nothing.

So did I sell at the point that Barclays had recovered to £3? No. Why? I try to sell shares as rarely as possible and I did so on this occasion only because even the consistent investor who takes a long-term view has a tolerance threshold for risk and has to protect their wealth. At the time I sold some shares in Barclays for £3, I did so only because the holding I had in Barclays was proportionately large in relation to my wider portfolio. Given the general uncertainty around banks, it seemed only sensible to reduce my exposure to the risk to an acceptable level to myself, and to do so rationally and for sound reasons. I did not know at the stage at which I sold how low Barclays share price would fall. As soon as I realised that it was falling way below anything that could be rationally justified or evidenced, I became very interested indeed in the business again and started to buy the shares back at an aggressive pace.

Some people will have admittedly piled into Barclays at the point at which the shares were selling at 60p and sold at over £3 for a major profit, and there is nothing wrong with that, but this kind of process is exceptionally rare and notoriously hard to judge even for the so-called 'experts'.

Throughout 2010 and probably beyond the share price of Barclays amongst others is likely to remain volatile. Applying some of the well established principles in this book will help you to exploit this volatility to your advantage.

So before anyone reading this thinks that lots of money can therefore be made quickly from quick buying and selling, the following points should be kept firmly at the forefront of your mind.

This example was used to illustrate a point about how a superior knowledge of your own character and tolerance for risk can reveal market opportunities that others, even experienced investors who should know better, will miss. I did NOT want to sell any shares in Barclays at all at any price. I did so as a result of a once-in-a-decade exceptional set of circumstances where it was prudent to do so.

INVESTING IS *NOT* SPECULATION

There is a difference between speculation and investing. I see the distinction as defined by the length of time over which the investor expects to realise their investment; or to put it another way, how quickly one expects to make money. Speculation to me is high-risk-get-rich-quick territory. Investing is managed risk over long periods of time where you can acquire wealth slowly. This book is about investing, not speculating, and I am an investor by nature, not a speculator. I am in it for the long haul, and having bought many Barclays shares for 60p, I intend to hang onto them. My view is that they will move yet higher over time.

The massive and largely unprecedented increase in the share price of Barclays was not anticipated by me or probably by many others. So did I get lucky? Well, yes and no. It was my view that the share price of Barclays would eventually recover and, whilst the past is no way of accurately predicting the future, I felt that it would rise to around the £3.20 mark in the medium term. The difference between my expectations and what happened is that I would have been happy for it to return to that price within five years. As it happened, it did so in less than five months.

WHAT CAN WE LEARN FROM THIS EXAMPLE?

I understood and *applied* my own tolerance to risk consistently and within my own framework. I did so dispassionately and rationally. I did not sell my Barclays shares at the earliest sign of problems in the banking industry and even when I did it was a calculated move that locked in only a marginal loss. I then waited and when the time was right in my view, ignoring all of the press and furore about banks, and hysteria about hidden debts and possible losses and the end of our entire economic system, I rationally applied a well-known secret that has been around for more than half a decade. The great Warren Buffet summed it up best when he said:

'Be greedy when others are fearful, and fearful when others are greedy.'

Warren Buffet

That is exactly why I bought back into Barclays at around 60p. Many people would now sell that same stock but I would argue that those people are not investors; they are speculators, and there is a big difference. The consistent investor will always take the long-term view; the speculator is looking to make a quick profit. Both approaches can work for you, but which one you take is up to you. For me, the long road is the one less travelled and the one I take because I think it works. For me, it is also the one most likely to pay dividends over time. Speculating to me is a form of gambling and not suited to my investment goals and personality, but you are not me and you may take a different path.

HOW WOULD YOU BEHAVE IN THIS EXAMPLE?

You should consider how you would behave were you to invest £10,000 only to see three months later, that its value has reduced to £6,000 and that there is every indication, at least in the press and even amongst speculators and your friends, that it may drop even further to say £4,000. What would you do? Sell? Hang on? Buy more? That is a key question for you to answer, and more importantly, understand why you answered as you did.

'Investing should be more like watching paint dry or watching grass grow. If you want excitement, take $800 and go to Las Vegas.'

Paul Samuelson – American Keynesian economist

The honest and considered answer to this dilemma should inform the guiding principles around how you behave in relation to your investing style. Nobody else can say what will work for you, but not understanding your own behaviours in stressful, confusing or ambiguous situations will not be conducive to a successful investing strategy where a considered and rational approach is required. Those with a short attention span who want to get rich quick and have a tendency for adrenalin-producing pursuits are unlikely to enjoy a successful investment career, despite the odd one or two who do and enjoy telling the world about it.

There is nothing wrong with anyone making money quickly, but there is danger in thinking it is an approach that can work for you. It is human nature to find these isolated examples appealing; after all, it is hard sometimes to be patient in a fast-moving world where the pace of change we are told is increasing constantly. However, I take the long-term view, much longer than I will be around to see in fact. I am thinking about the kind of world my grandchildren will live in, and what that might be (my son is currently two years old.)

CAN YOU SEE THE BIGGER PICTURE?

The person capable of standing back may notice that change is the one constant, so whilst everyone is throwing around commonly-held views as though they are 'facts', one might do well to stand back and consider whether a perceived truth is indeed so, or whether in fact the more things apparently change, the more some things do indeed remain the same.

Following the crowd and abandoning a commitment to a long-term approach in a business you bought into believing it to be sound could lead to a real loss, especially if, six months later, it turns out that the crowd consisted of ill-informed speculating lemmings and now the shares you sold have doubled in value as sanity returned to the market.

'An optimist will tell you the glass is half-full; the pessimist, half-empty; and the engineer will tell you the glass is twice the size it needs to be.'

Author unknown

The importance of understanding your own behaviours in relation to your actions cannot be over-stated. Once understood, you will be able to apply your preferred investing style consistently without emotional or psychological bias. Something which is easier said than done.

KNOW-IT-ALLS HAVE A LOT TO LEARN

One of the biggest dangers with investing is over-confidence or the addictive nature of doing well. This is hard-wired into human beings. It is all about maintaining a sense of perspective, and sometimes we need to remind ourselves that we should guard against over-confidence as much as risk aversion. You never know as much as you think you do.

Always try and see things from a new or different perspective. It can be quite developmental. The following tale may seem a little out of place in a book about investing in the stock market. I think it belongs perfectly.

Consider the following tale

Don't we all

I was parked in front of the mall wiping off my car. I had just come from the car wash and was waiting for my wife to get out of work.

Coming my way from across the parking lot was what society would consider a bum. From the looks of him, he had no car, no home, no clean clothes, and no money. There are times when you feel generous but there are other times that you just don't want to be bothered. This was one of those 'don't want to be bothered' times.

'I hope he doesn't ask me for any money,' I thought. He didn't. He came and sat on the curb in front of the bus stop, but he didn't look like he could have enough money to even ride the bus.

After a few minutes he spoke. 'That's a very pretty car,' he said.

He was ragged but he had an air of dignity around him. His scraggly blond beard kept more than his face warm. I said, 'Thanks', and continued wiping off my car.

He sat there quietly as I worked. The expected plea for money never came. As the silence between us widened, something inside said, 'Ask him if he needs any help'. I was sure that he would say 'Yes' but I held true to the inner voice.

'Do you need any help?' I asked. He answered in three simple words:

'Don't we all?'

Author unknown

WHAT CAN WE LEARN FROM THIS SIMPLE TALE?

I like this tale because it reminds me of the importance of seeing things from different perspectives. It is very hard sometimes to see something from a perspective that is opposite to your intrinsic nature, but it is essential. Our own perceptions of ourselves can be both deceiving and highly dangerous to the investor.

Remember that investing is a constant learning process, and never start to believe you have it sussed or allow a small success to seem like something other than it is. Many investors can lose what they have gained from this very process. If you do well, take a step back and reflect. You have not discovered a system that works or have a profound gift for investing. Rather you are learning, and you will need to see both your successes and failures as part of the same process. It is about thinking differently to gain an unfair advantage, and that is what we will explore next.

CHAPTER 3:

Think like a machine

HOW TO TAKE EMOTION OUT OF INVESTING

'There seems to be some perverse human characteristic that likes to make easy things difficult.'

Warren Buffett – investor

Where investing is concerned, being human means that it is highly likely you are your own worst enemy. This may sound odd but bear with me. Everyone has the same challenge to overcome. The solution is to know how to win the battle against your own psychological biases and emotional reactions, or at least control them to an extent that is beneficial to your investment approach, and to do so in such a way that sets you apart from most other people who cannot. After all, if everyone could do this, there would be no competitive advantage in doing so and everyone would buy shares in winning companies thus limiting future growth potential in the share price. The good news is that most people fail to do this. Make yourself an exception and you have cracked a major challenge.

As Buffet has suggested, it is indeed something perverse about human nature that makes it so hard to follow what should be easy steps in investing, and sticking to it. Thinking that you will not panic should markets and your share prices tumble is one thing, but doing it is quite another. Most people do not master this basic principle and most people do the opposite of what you should do, which is to buy your chosen share at a good price (as close to a bargain as possible) and at some future point, should you wish to realise your profit, sell at a higher price.

Sadly human folly tends to override our rational investment objectives and, more often than not, we buy high and sell low. You can see this

*'Most of the time common stocks are subject
to irrational and excessive price fluctuations
in both directions as the consequence of the
ingrained tendency of most people to speculate
or gamble . . . to give way to hope, fear and
greed.'*

Benjamin Graham – American economist

pattern in share prices and the volumes traded in certain shares all
of the time, but especially during times of increased volatility such as
during the latter part of 2008 and the first half of 2009.

HOW EMOTIONS IMPACT ON OUR INVESTING JUDGEMENT

Our emotional and psychological responses to investing are significant.
Much has been written on this subject and it is not my intention to go
over ground already covered but a few key issues are worth noting.

Firstly, good results have less of an impact emotionally than bad
ones. A declining share price can lead to panic, stress, and irrational
behaviours of many types. This is when you are most likely to sell at
a loss. Above all, you should guard against this and remind yourself
of what you set out to do and why you bought the share in the first
place. We will cover that in more detail later, but panic and affording
media hysteria more credit than it is worth can be a costly mistake. The
media know very well that bad news sells better than good news, but
that doesn't mean it is true or warrants any greater attention. When
things seem really bad, remember that they may only seem that way. It
may not actually be so.

Secondly, a couple of good results can encourage your ego to run riot.
It is all too easy to start thinking that you have a gift, a talent that
gives you a privileged insight into the workings of the market that
only you and Warren Buffet share. This mistake can be as dangerous as
the previous one. Remember this: anyone can buy a tennis racket, but
make you Martina Navratilova, it does not.

The art of investment is just that. A skill that takes more than a lifetime to learn. This will be discussed in more detail towards the end of this book, but it is worth bearing in mind. We can all buy that tennis racket; it is the same piece of equipment to anyone, but we will all use it slightly differently. Some will rise to excellence, some will use it competently, and some will never really use it at all.

With investing what is likely to make the difference for you is your capacity to learn how to manage your emotions and make your psychological biases behave in a certain way under certain circumstances. This process is much the same as that which an athlete trains by, working both mentally and physically to achieve their goals.

> *'Emotions are your worst enemy in the stock market.'*
>
> Don Hays – investor

STICK TO YOUR PLAN

It is worth pausing at this point to reflect on that and to note that it is easy to say it, another to do it. Those who can stick to a plan in the face of much adversity are far more likely to achieve their mission, as are those who have a well thought-out plan in the first place.

An example of how sticking to a plan can be more problematic than you expected

Belling the Cat

The mice once called a meeting to decide on a plan to free themselves of their enemy, the cat. At least they wished to find some way of knowing when she was coming, so they might have time to run away. Indeed, something had to be done, for they lived in such constant fear of her claws that they hardly dared stir from their dens by night or day.

Many plans were discussed, but none of them was thought good enough. At last a very young mouse got up and said, 'I have a plan that seems very simple, but I know it will be successful. All we have to do is to hang a bell about the cat's neck. When we hear the bell ringing we will know immediately that our enemy is coming.'

All the mice were much surprised that they had not thought of such a plan before. But in the midst of the rejoicing over their good fortune, an old mouse arose and said, 'I will say that the plan of the young mouse is very good, but let me ask one question: who will bell the Cat?'

Moral: 'It is one thing to say that something should be done, but quite a different matter to do it.'

Aesop fable

UNDERSTAND HOW YOUR EMOTIONS IMPACT ON BEHAVIOUR AND HOW YOU CAN START TO MODIFY YOUR RESPONSE

It is easy to say you should control your emotions against panic, as it is easy to come up with a plan, but sometimes our emotions and predispositions to certain behaviours can impact on our actions. Even the most experienced and best investors in the world can succumb to this as they are, mostly, human after all; it is just that they do it less often than most. Remove emotion from your investing decisions and base them on a consistent set of sound principles, and you will be off to a good start.

The internet has made a wealth of investing intelligence easily available to the investor; it is how we make sense of it, and our psychological and emotional reaction to it, that determine our actions in investing in terms of what shares we buy and why.

This has been the bedrock on which some of the world's most successful investors have built their fortune, which incidentally, most have achieved over a relatively long period of time. The world of quick wins belongs to gambling and speculation, not investment, and I didn't see too many winners in Vegas when I was there, except for the casino itself of course.

There are some characteristics that are certainly beneficial to the consistent investor, patience, tenacity and commitment being three important ones.

A BIT ABOUT RISK

A significant element of any approach to investing is your appetite for, or rather capacity to manage, risk. Risk touches nearly every element of investing in much the same way as it does our daily lives, and therefore it will be discussed throughout this book although many writers would dedicate a specific chapter to it.

I don't see the point in isolating risk to a specific chapter. It is illogical to do so as risk is embedded in almost everything. Crossing the road carries a risk, as does flying on a plane or eating soft cheese.

Risk is inherent in everything from the price you pay for a share, to how much money you have in cash assets, to your age, to your lifestyle and so on. Anyone who has completed an insurance application form recently will know how many factors your insurance company regards as associated with risk. Since risk runs throughout nearly every aspect of investing it would seem rather odd to isolate it to one stand-alone chapter. It will be highlighted where especially relevant but for now it should be noted that pretty much everything has an element of risk, and that in understanding and managing risk and our approach to it we can use it to our significant advantage. Most people do not know how to manage their exposure to risk. Master this and you can equip yourself with an unfair advantage.

Investing, like life, is very much about gaining an unfair advantage, and it can be surprising how you achieve it.

CHAPTER 4:

The journey begins

THE SOONER YOUR START, THE LUCKIER YOU SEEM TO GET

The whole point of investing in the stock market and buying shares is to improve your financial position and help to realise your financial objectives, whatever they might be. It can also be a lot of fun. No, really, it can.

'The journey is the reward.'

Chinese proverb

Although this is very much an arguable point and a generalisation, the stock market, for most ordinary people, represents the best way of achieving their financial goals and aspirations given that most savings accounts pay only a modest return even in times when interest rates are favourable. Good investments combined with time are the best recipe for improving your future wealth. Sometimes I look at my two-year-old boy and think just how much he could compound if he started investing now, and how cute he looks as well, of course.

Picking a good stock at a bargain price that pays dividends can significantly out-perform most other forms of investments broadly speaking, especially if the share price increases over time beyond expectations.

LEARN FROM PEOPLE WHO ARE BETTER THAN YOU

Warren Buffet is not just generally regarded as the greatest living investor in the world, but he is equally well known for his wisdom and some of his sayings. One of his well-known sayings is 'Rule number one, never lose money; and rule number two, don't forget rule number one'. This quote should be taken as tongue-in-cheek rather than literally since Buffet himself has not managed to avoid losing money, as his investment in Conoco-Phillips revealed. Even a master such as Buffet can make an obvious mistake, in that case buying into an oil company when prices were at a peak and in the face of a looming recession. It cost him a lot of money at that time, although it has since recovered somewhat.

Such mistakes, however, are rare. Buffet has learned over a long investing career what works for him and what doesn't, and he has stuck to his approach through times of adversity and prosperity earning him worldwide respect. Whilst it would be foolish to attempt to mirror his approach, much can be learned from studying the investing behaviour of people like Warren Buffet.

BE REALISTIC

Before we move on to more detailed commentary on some of the criteria worth considering when looking at a particular stock, it is worth reflecting on what your objectives are and why you wish to embark on an investment journey at all.

Having a clear sense of what you realistically expect to achieve will help you to focus on what types of shares you may wish to buy, and having already considered what type of investing personality you are, what behaviours to be aware of and what your risk tolerance is, you

Alice, 'Would you tell me, please, which way I ought to go from here?'

'That depends a good deal on where you want to get to,' said the Cat.

'I don't much care where,' said Alice.

'Then it doesn't matter which way you go,' said the Cat.

Alice in Wonderland, 1951

can start to search for your first investments with a clear sense of why your are going down a particular road.

If you do not have a clear sense of what you wish to achieve, it will be much more likely that you will make a less than optimum choice of investments and that you may become disillusioned with what you achieve. By that point you are one step away from selling at a loss and before you know it – well, you get the picture. Be modest in your ambitions and realistic about what can be achieved. Do not expect to be right 100% of the time. Anything over 50% of the time and you are doing well. One of the key skills to learn is a little about how to understand and appreciate a business, and not the share price. This approach will serve you well and we will look at that next.

CHAPTER 5:

Understand the business – not the share price

UNDERSTAND A LITTLE ABOUT THE BUSINESS, NOT THE STOCK MARKET

'Rule No.1: Never lose money. Rule No.2: Never forget rule No.1.'

Warren Buffett – investor

Try and see the business from the inside out, not just the outside in. Today's winners can become tomorrow's losers. This is why it is critical to understand the nature of the business, far more than the share price (as previously outlined, the share price can occasionally, although not always, have more to do with irrational behaviour and passing storms than business reality).

I pay relatively little initial attention to the current share price, although it is important, and we shall explore that later. Rather, the first stage when considering buying a particular stock is to ask yourself, 'How well do you understand the business?'

Really understanding a business can be a lengthy process and as complex as you want to make it. Start by thinking about some relatively basic questions. What sector does it operate in? Warren Buffet has tended to avoid sectors

'For every complex problem there is a simple solution that is wrong.'

G.B. Shaw, 1856–1950 – Irish critic and poet

such as technology stocks with a good reason, in that he claims not to understand them.

For my part, I have done similar in that I have never been able to work out why on earth the share price of Google is so consistently high. Yes, it is technically worth a lot of money and is a smart business and has significant brand value, but it has, at least to me, an obvious Achilles heel in that it seems to be overly reliant on online advertising revenues and its current technical competitive advantage. Will Google still be doing so well in 20 years? Maybe, but I doubt it. I suspect that it will diversify into many different media-related businesses in order to manage its own risk and continue to grow. I do not fully understand Google and therefore it would be foolish for me to consider it as an investment even if the rest of the world regards it as a great buy (which it seems to, so make up your own mind).

In the knowledge economy your economic moat can be drained quickly, especially in the internet business. I may, of course, be wrong and Google may, ten years from now, own the internet and everything else, but for me it represents a bad risk, not because of the business itself but because of my awareness of my own limitations. I am a bad risk for Google, rather than the other way round, so I avoid it. I am most definitely in the minority with my view about Google, but if Buffet has avoided it, then I am in good company. I have also avoided buying shares in what I regard as general retailers on the high street, businesses like Marks and Spencer and Next and Debenhams and so on. I do not understand the general world of retailing and so it is outside my sphere of competence. The exception I made to this was when I bought into Game Group shares but that was an isolated case of a retail business that I did indeed understand.

YOU NEED ONLY A BASIC UNDERSTANDING AT FIRST

The point is, do you understand the sector on a basic level? This can be as simple as people will always need to eat, so supermarkets are likely to stick around and the likes of Tesco are unlikely to go bust anytime soon. If you have a low to medium appetite for risk, a business like

Tesco can represent a solid buy at the right time for the right price (I would recommend waiting for a passing storm, like some temporary media frenzy to dent the share price and then buy, although, of course, you may be waiting a long time).

LOOK AT WHO IS RUNNING THE BUSINESS

You should also consider who is running the company and what their reputation is. The CV of many executives of public companies are available online and a little research can often reveal a lot about the background and management style of the people running the company that you are considering buying.

Be wary of marketing spin and empty rhetoric. Look for the facts. What has the management actually achieved and delivered over time?

'You can't build a reputation on what you are going to do.'

Henry Ford – founder of the Ford Motor Company

You should also be wary of excessive remuneration for senior executives which can be indicative of a business culture where managers are working for managers, not in the best interests of the shareholder or the future of the business itself. No matter how big the enterprise this can spell disaster. Quality leaders will rarely take excessive bonuses and outrageous rewards. Many of the best entrepreneurs are motivated by factors other than money, such as the desire to do things their own way, create wealth, grow something, and own something worthwhile, and their mission is a noble one.

'People are definitely a company's greatest asset. It doesn't make any difference whether the product is cars or cosmetics. A company is only as good as the people it keeps.'

Mary Kay Ash – American businesswoman

YOU DON'T NEED TO BE AN ACCOUNTANT TO UNDERSTAND IF A BUSINESS IS GROWING

There are some simple measures to look at. They may not make much sense at first but in a short time they will. Pay attention to some of the basic finances of a business. You would be well advised to seek out and investigate businesses that have a good return on the capital employed and ideally with relatively little debt. I tend to avoid companies with more than 35% net gearing (debt) on their books (*this can be easily located on the fundamentals of the business which you will be able to access from any online share-dealing service or direct from the company website itself*).

Company statements, annual statements, market updates and annual reports and so on should be easy to understand, although often they are not. Be wary if such reports are written in a less-than-accessible manner. I also recommend that you read them backwards, by which I mean start at the end and work back as these documents have a tendency to try and bury anything less than positive in sections that most normal people would not bother, or rather have the stamina, to read. If you can start to think like a machine and carry on after most would not, you may just find something that stops you making a costly mistake. If you can't understand it, it is probably quite deliberately opaque, and you should exercise appropriate caution.

'Experience taught me a few things. One is to listen to your gut, no matter how good something sounds on paper. The second is that you're generally better off sticking with what you know. And the third is that sometimes your best investments are the ones you don't make.'

Donald Trump – American businessman

LOOK FOR GROWTH

Does the company have strong cash flow and have its profits been increasing consistently? If not, why not? Whilst the past is no prediction of the future, once again caution should be exercised with regard to any business that cannot demonstrate what appears to be consistent growth. I have always been amazed at how many investors buy shares in companies that have both not made a profit and/or not shown consistent growth. Almost daily I see so-called experts providing stock 'tips' often in companies that have never made a penny! Yes, they may do so in future, but such purchases and 'advice' should be avoided by a mile by the consistent investor and left to the realms of traders and speculators and those with a capacity for very high risk and who have very deep pockets. Would you lend money to someone with no income, or at least, not enough to pay it back? Banks did that and look what happened.

BRAND VALUE

Does the company have strong brand value? I have shares in the Harley Davidson company which is one of the world's most recognised brands, so much so that many of the people who buy their products have a Harley Davidson tattoo on their body. That kind of brand value and loyalty provides a company with considerable defence against a passing storm, and also enables the company to reflect this value in its pricing policy.

KNOW A LITTLE ABOUT WHAT YOU ARE GETTING INTO

Does the company require a genius to run it and do you understand it?

An example to prove that we all make mistakes

As proof that it is harder to practise what one preaches, my one instance in ten years of buying shares in a company that I neither understood, nor really liked, was a biotechnology company called

Tepnel Life Sciences. To this day I have no idea how I came to own shares in that company as, looking back, it should have failed almost every personal test I should have applied to it, but own it I did.

I bought the shares for around 10p and sold them for 26.75p a year later. A nice return you might think, but this was more by chance than design, and by 'more' I mean completely. I didn't really know what I was doing and should have avoided this investment like a politician avoids an answer. The business was taken over on 8 April 2009 by Gen-Probe, a world leader in molecular diagnostics, and due to the takeover, the share price soared despite the company not having made any significant money whatsoever to that point.

Before you judge me too harshly on not following my own advice, even Warren Buffet can make mistakes and forget everything he knows, as demonstrated by buying Conoco-Phillips when he did, what Buffet now refers to as his 'major mistake'. In my case, at least I made a nice profit and promised myself not to be tempted again by things I don't understand.

The reason I provide this example is that unless you are a scientist in a relevant area, you are unlikely to understand exactly what it is that made Tepnel Life Sciences worth buying. Stick to what you know and can understand.

WHAT DO YOU LIKE TO BUY?

It is worth noting what you buy yourself and what you don't. If you like something, the chances are, so will other people. Take a moment to reflect on the behaviour of people and buying patterns you see next time you are wandering down the high street. Stopping for a moment to reflect on how people behave in towns and cities can be quite revealing, especially if a company you are interested in buying has a High Street presence.

Recently I have noticed how there is an almost-permanent queue in Greggs the bakers. Affordable, quick and consistent snacks are unlikely to go out of fashion and the dominance of Greggs on the high street in the UK in terms of size provides it with a solid foundation and defence against changing fortunes.

NOTICE WHAT OTHER PEOPLE SPEND MONEY ON

An example to illustrate the point

I noticed recently how the relative volume of people in the software and hardware retailer GAME seems to have declined, at least, purely from an observational point of view at that particular time. I have been into those stores on many occasions, and shop there myself, and yet I have noticed how their shops appear to be much quieter of late. This might just be due to the cyclical nature of the console market, or it could be an alarm signal for the potential investor. My main concern with GAME would be their long-term strategy given the big unknown of online gaming. How GAME shops would continue to thrive in a downloadable world is very unclear to me, especially looking ten or 20 years down the line when it is likely that a much larger proportion of the world, and especially the UK, will have access to faster broadband. We will explore Game Group in more detail later.

THE PAST IS SO MUCH EASIER TO PREDICT

A couple of further points worth considering in understanding a potential investment is whether the earnings of the business are relatively predictable or likely to be highly volatile. It is relatively easier to invest in something where the projected earnings are likely to have a strong element of stability about them.

DO THE PEOPLE RUNNING THE BUSINESS HAVE THE OWNER'S EYE?

Does the management of the business have a significant investment and commitment to the enterprise in the medium to long term without owning too large a stake? This can be a significant issue where a business has one or two shareholders with very large stakes in a business. On the one hand, it can signify commitment, but on the other, it can pose a significant risk to the potential small investor.

'Investors have very short memories.'

Roman Abramovich – Russian investor

As a general rule, my advice would be to avoid this type of business and look for one where the shareholders represent a diversified group with no one party holding too much of the business. The same principle would apply to your own portfolio, owning too much of one thing can be a very bad thing as many people around the year 2000 discovered. Owning shares in many different businesses is a good idea as long as they are great businesses in different sectors, and not all in, say, the technology sector.

Learn from the past. It is amazing how many people fail to do this. I think it is forgivable to make a new mistake, but to make the same mistakes in new ways is not.

INVESTORS DON'T GET EXCITED, THEY GET SATISFACTORY RESULTS

Our human desire for excitement or prejudicial biases towards certain behaviours can make us become an easy victim for the latest 'tip' on a new 'exciting emergent opportunity' or the 'must have' gadget etc. How many times do you hear the phrase 'nobody could have predicted'? In many cases where the economic fortunes of the world are concerned, this is absolutely nonsense.

Whilst you should limit your audience with loud individuals who make apparently-convincing claims about exactly what is going to happen to world markets or business, some things are very predictable if you can control your emotions and think clearly.

THIS TIME IT'S NOT DIFFERENT

Trends in the stock market can be cyclical. Be aware of this. Property prices can follow trends as those bying a house around 2000 and selling it around 2007 will know. At different times the prices of things can be relatively cheap or expensive. A house in 2000 seems cheap by today's prices, but did it seem that way back then? The principles of how you judge the relative cost of an investment remain the same, so remember that this time it's not different.

LEARN FROM THE PAST AND LOOK TO THE FUTURE, AS THAT IS WHERE WE ARE ALL GOING

The key point is to learn from the past and whilst it is no prediction of future patterns and behaviour, it can help in working out whether something is likely to be over-priced in relation to wider trends and intelligence. I wonder how long it will be before we see the re-emergence of sub-prime lending, albeit under a new badge and from a new breed of banks? Ten, maybe 15 or 20 years? Who knows, but once again, when it happens I won't be surprised and I, for one, won't be investing then either.

These are just some of the initial key factors you may wish to look into in assessing a business, and represent just the tip of the iceberg. The more you look into and research a business, the more you will understand where it has come from and get a feel for where you think it might be going.

Let's look in more detail at how we may begin selecting shares to buy, and no, I don't make any 'tips' or recommendations.

CHAPTER 6:

Selecting your shares

'It's tough to make predictions,
especially about the future.'

Yogi Berra – baseball player and commentator

You should not waste too much time trying to predict the unpredictable. Whilst we can learn lessons from the past, the past is no prediction of the future. Someone once said that trying to predict the future by looking at the past was akin to trying to drive a car by looking through the rear view mirror. You would do well to remember that when considering a particular stock.

This book assumes that you are looking to invest in individual shares and that you will exercise your own judgement and accountability in doing so. However, it is worth noting that for many investors this is neither a desirable nor appropriate way of achieving their financial aims via the stock market. Many would be wise to put their money into bonds or investment vehicles that automatically select a basket of best-of-breed companies, and this requires both little maintenance or stress on the part of the investor. There is also a body of evidence to suggest that this course of action can deliver very comparable results to any other approach.

You would be well advised to get some truly independent advice as to what style of investing is appropriate for you and your objectives, and remember when taking advice, if you are not paying for it, someone else is. Caution is always your ally.

That said, this book will assume that you are at the stage where investing in the stock market directly and hand picking your own shares has been the selected investment option. For me, this has always been preferable since I trust my own judgement and I am prepared to exercise it with accountability, as aware as I can be of my own strengths, weaknesses and prejudices.

THERE'S A LOT OF DATA OUT THERE AND NOT MUCH INTELLIGENCE

There is a huge amount of data and information available from online share dealing facilities, and most tend to offer very similar and comparable services. Once you have set yourself up with your own online share dealing service, you will have access to a whole range of stock screening services and data on a given share. Take some time to familiarise yourself with the format of this data before starting to dig deeper into what you want to know. It is how you interpret and make sense of this data, and what actions you take from it, that potentially turns it from data into something more strategically useful like intelligence.

Most of the data is not that relevant, but there are some simple measures certainly worth considering as a starting point to further investigation and these will be explored throughout the rest of this book.

For this part, let's consider some guiding principles in starting to think about selecting some contenders for your portfolio.

ARE THINGS REALLY HOW THEY SEEM?

Firstly, it may seem obvious, but stick to what you know, or at least, feel that you understand.

> '*The stock market is filled with individuals who know the price of everything, but the value of nothing.*'
>
> Philip Fisher – investor

We will discuss that issue in more detail later, but consider this. Following the crowd or a pattern of behaviour can sometimes be a big mistake. Had I done so in early 2009, I would not have bought banking shares at a time when others were selling.

When you think that everyone else knows something but you just can't see it yourself, reflect on this and do more research. Are share prices behaving irrationally? Could the real picture be very different from what it seems? Are people behaving with a particular bias because of negative and recent events and is this clouding their investing judgement?

An example to illustrate the point, and it has a frog in it again

A group of frogs was travelling through the woods, and two of them fell into a deep pit.

When the other frogs saw how deep the pit was, they told the two frogs that they were as good as dead.

The two frogs ignored the comments and tried to jump up out of the pit with all their might. The other frogs kept telling them to stop, that they were as good as dead.

Finally, one of the frogs took heed to what the other frogs were saying and gave up. He fell down and died.

The other frog continued to jump as hard as he could. Once again, the crowd of frogs yelled at him to stop the pain and just die. He jumped even harder and finally got out.

When he got out, the other frogs said, 'Did you not hear us?'

The frog explained to them that he was deaf. He thought they were encouraging him the entire time.

Author unknown

It really can pay dividends to see things differently sometimes and to go against the grain.

IT'S HOW YOU USE A TOOL THAT MATTERS

Most online investment facilities provide a range of quite simple tools such as heat maps or share screening tools to help you to identify shares that are behaving in certain ways, tailored to your own preferences. This can be a useful starting point in identifying companies that you may wish to consider

'I was able to see what I wanted to do, I could see the opportunity, even when others could not, and I stayed committed to doing it and doing it well, no matter what.'

Magic Johnson – basketball player

investing in. I use these tools from time to time, most notably during a period of volatility as I look for companies that may be trading well below what I believe to be their real value. During times of crisis when most people are losing their heads and behaving irrationally is when the consistent investor can seize the best opportunities.

It requires patience and some work, but it can pay the highest dividends to those with the tenacity to stick at it.

'The Chinese use two brush strokes to write the word "crisis". One brush stroke stands for danger; the other for opportunity. In a crisis, be aware of the danger – but recognize the opportunity.'

John F. Kennedy – former US President

KEEP IT SIMPLE

In selecting the businesses that you may consider investing in, you should not feel overwhelmed by a lack of experience or knowledge of technical analysis. From my experience, some relatively basic research and rudimentary measures are sufficient. If there was a scientific formula for picking winning companies that actually worked, the world of investing would be very different. Despite some of the finest minds the planet has to offer attempting to produce such a formula, system or strategy, there is no such thing to this day. Anyone pretending there is should be regarded with a healthy dose of cynicism.

'The investor of today does not profit from yesterday's growth.'

Warren Buffett – investor

The main question is, can you read? If you can, and presumably you can if you are reading this, then that is a great start. If you can combine your ability to read information with a bit of a talent for business literacy, by which I mean disseminating what is relevant and informative from what is marketing nonsense and creative accountancy, then that is also a great start. If not, don't worry, you can pick it up quickly.

Finally, the types of companies that different people like to buy into is as varied as people themselves. What is interesting to one person is dull to another, and what looks like a great investment to one person would not to many others. Therefore this book makes no attempt at recommending any particular sector or share. Rather I will use a few examples of what I have bought over the years, or haven't, to illustrate a few points, and highlight some approaches which have worked for me.

WHAT WORKS FOR ONE, MAY NOT WORK FOR ANOTHER

My approach may not work for you, but hopefully this book will provide some signposts on a particular view or position from which you can decide how to chart your own course. The key point is that this book should support you in thinking more critically about where to place your money and in doing so also increase your chances of a positive result.

Before moving on to some specific measures that I think are worthy of your consideration, it might be useful to provide an actual example of a company that I hold shares in, and illustrate some of the reasons why I hold it.

'Your choices are half chance; so are everybody else's.'

Baz Luhrmann – film director

The company is the Harley Davidson motorcycle company. In my view, this is a great business, but I waited a long time to invest in it. The following example highlights a number of key issues that you should consider when looking to invest in a business, and highlights the importance of your personality type and personality traits in relation to successful investing.

Patience really is a virtue. In the world of investing, it is the tortoise that always wins the race.

CHAPTER 7:

Time is your ally – the Harley Davidson example

'Life begins at 30 but it doesn't get really interesting until around 150.'

Author unknown

WITH INVESTING, THE MORE TIME YOU HAVE, THE BETTER IT GETS

The following example will illustrate how patience combined with timing can pay off.

Harley Davidson is, in my view, a special company. I have been interested in the Harley Davidson company for a long time and waited many years (it felt like very long years) before buying shares in this business, finally in early 2009. I had wanted to buy shares in Harley Davidson for nearly five years prior to that date, but, as is often the case in investing, time is your ally. I will not pretend that it was easy to resist buying them earlier and many times I was tempted to, but the correct course of action was to be consistent with my investment principles and it was the right thing to do.

Wait until the time is right, and when you think it is, invest aggressively. A little research online will reveal many contrasting viewpoints as to whether it is best to invest a little and often, or one large sum once. From my experience it is a bit of both and not too much of either. It is always a good idea to have some disposable cash available so that when the opportunity arises after your patient wait, you can fully exploit it to the best of your ability.

43

That is what I did in the case of Harley Davidson. Consider the following.

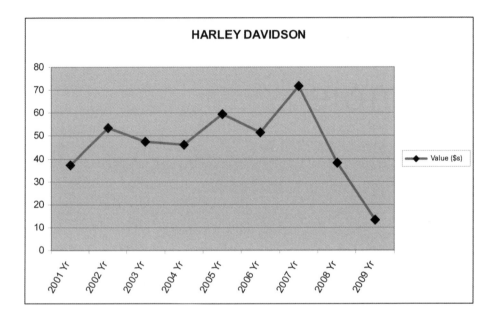

Fig. 2 Share price of Harley Davidson company 2001–2009

As you can see from the chart, the share price of the Harley Davidson company over the past nine years or so was showing broadly consistent growth hitting a high in 2007 of broadly $72 a share, with the average price between 2000 and 2009 being around $45 a share.

Remember that looking at historical share price trends is useful only in the sense that it provides you with some historical context for the current price. Remember that the past is no indication of likely future prices.

What it does provide you with is a view as to whether, in a historical context, the current price is above or below the historical average. How you interpret that and what weight you apply to it is up to you, and you should form your judgement in connection with a range of other indicators and wider research. Some people would be happy to buy a share that may be at its highest point in its history if they feel strongly enough that it will go higher still. Others may avoid a share in that situation and seek out those which appear to offer better value in the share price against its historical patterns. There is no right or wrong answer here. It is about your personal preference.

VOLATILITY AND CHAOS ARE GOOD FOR THE INVESTOR

During late 2008 and 2009, share markets across the world starting to behave in a very volatile way as the widely-debated economic crisis started to hit home. Throughout 2010 we have already seen this volatility continue as the debt crisis impacts on confidence. This impacted on many different types of companies, and continues to do so, but companies in the motor industry and the finance sector were affected particularly strongly. However, just because General Motors may be making too many cars that people don't seem to want or at least are willing to buy, doesn't mean that a company such as Harley Davidson should be viewed in the same context. In the motor industry it is, but a very different animal it is too, and this had seemingly escaped the notice of most other people. I could sense that an opportunity may be on the horizon.

People were behaving irrationally and a company that was superb in my view was starting to become very under-valued, and it wasn't only me who noticed. When the share price of Harley Davidson hit around $8 a share in early 2009, I invested in it aggressively and my five-year wait was over.

Within a few months the share price had risen significantly and in early 2010 had risen to the $27–$30 range. As a consistent investor, I am not selling my shares in this company despite the fact that I could have realised a significant profit. My holding period is always intended to be forever and this would change only under a particular set of exceptional circumstances. In the past ten years I have sold shares on only several occasions, and all of those occurred during 2008 and were related to the finance sector. I think that Harley Davidson shares are worth far more than the current $23 price. If I could, I would buy the entire company.

WHY WAS I SO INTERESTED IN HARLEY DAVIDSON?

Later in this book I will outline some of the specific measures I use when looking at a business as an investment proposition, but I wanted to provide the Harley Davidson example early on to illustrate a few key points that I think are especially significant, as they are factors that you won't see on any normal technical analysis, balance sheet or similar economic or accounting measure.

> *'I am no longer an advocate of elaborate techniques of security analysis in order to find superior value opportunities.'*
>
> Benjamin Graham – American economist

As a consistent investor, time is your ally. Patience is your foundation and boredom is good once you have bought into a company. Consistent investing is not short-term excitement. If you feel you are more suited to short-term speculation and quick wins, there is nothing wrong with that *per se*, but the chances of you realising your long-term financial goals that way are not good. The odds are most definitely not in your favour.

I don't mean to keep banging on about Warren Buffet, but given his success, he is without a doubt a great example of how it should be done, and he has often commented on how stock market price movements are of relatively-little interest to him. I agree with that entirely. No matter how tempting it might be to check your share prices regularly, it can be a dangerous game. You should consider how you would feel if there was no daily share price movements and having bought the stock of your choice, the next update you would receive would be in ten-year intervals? If that concept makes you question what you are doing or pause to reflect, you should go back to chapter 1 and start again.

Taking a long-term view

Chances are if you are not sure about investing in a company for ten years, it is probably not the right stock for you, assuming you are in agreement with the core arguments of this book. An investor takes a long-term view, of more than five years. If your horizon is generally less than that then you may be more suited to speculation than investing. Once again there is nothing wrong with that, but it is a quite different approach from the one advocated here.

I waited a long time to buy Harley Davidson shares and despite wanting to buy them, I didn't until the time was, for me, right. This required discipline and faith in my conviction that the opportunity would arrive during a long period of time where there was no evidence whatsoever that the opportunity would come. I also had worked out what for me was an appropriate or good price for this company which was around the $18 mark, although of course as it turned out I got them for a lot less than that, which was very satisfactory indeed.

In case you are wondering how I arrived at the $18 figure, it was nothing scientific at all. It was merely a figure that I regarded as below any ten-year share price for the company and which seemed likely to be achievable in my judgement of what was about to happen to the world economy and the motor industry. Just as with the banks, whilst many motor companies were following less-than-efficient models or robust management practices, there were one or two exceptions in both industries that should not have been viewed in the same light, but that is indeed what happened with Harley Davidson.

Researching the company
I had also significantly researched the company. This process is something that I consider to be very important. Learn as much as you can about what it is that you are considering buying into. I understood that it had a powerful brand and a deeply loyal customer base. Many people who buy its products carry a tattoo of the company logo on their bodies. More than that, the company is very much a part of American culture and represents something about the American Dream, of freedom, rebellion and the open road. People feel both passionately and sentimentally about these qualities, and that represents powerful brand loyalty which can be a defence against challenging and changing times. Harley Davidson is one of the most

recognised brands in the world and that provides the company with a strong defence in times of adversity.

However, the company was not, and is not, perfect. It remains overly-reliant on a particular type of customer, in my view, and had a less than stellar 2008 in terms of costs and revenue. That said, it was trimming its workforce and costs, and underneath what I deemed to be a temporary storm, was hopefully a very solid business indeed. What is more, my personal view is that, as we head into a period of ten years of probable oil price volatility which will ultimately head upwards, I can see sales of motorcycles only increasing, but that is my personal subjective viewpoint only, not a recommendation about the future success of this or any other motorcycle company.

One final key factor in deciding to buy into the company was that Warren Buffet also did so in the form of lending the Harley Davidson company around $300 million. Whether this is good news or not for the company itself in the short to medium term is debatable, but what interested me was that Warren Buffet and his Berkshire Hathaway vehicle were willing to inject $300 million into the company in the first place.

Mr Buffet is not known for making speculative bets or losing money. Either Warren Buffet thinks that the Harley Davidson company is good for the money, or he thinks it isn't and he wants a much larger stake in it for a bargain price, but either way his actions warrant attention. For me, it was a positive not a negative action, although it may well have a negative material impact on the ability of the company to pay dividends in the short term, and some of its shareholders will not be happy about the terms and conditions of the loan. For me, however, there is a bigger picture.

Future of the company
My long-term view is that the Harley Davidson company will continue to do well, and has a solid future. It is undergoing a period of significant change and volatility but Buffet does not part with his money lightly. For me, it was a great buy at $8, but a much more risky

one at $23, and that is why time was my ally. If you are patient and disciplined enough, opportunities will reward the consistent investor.

'If you took our top 15 decisions out, we'd have a pretty average record. It wasn't hyperactivity, but a hell of a lot of patience. You stuck to your principles and when opportunities came along, you pounced on them with vigor.'

Charlie Munger – Vice Chairman, Berkshire Hathaway

HOW MUCH IS ENOUGH?

As mentioned previously, there are many different and contrasting views about whether it is better to invest a little and often, or invest larger sums occasionally. I think you should aim to do both differentially based on the state of the market at any given point. Once again, it is a matter for your personal judgement. Nobody can tell you or predict how you should behave in this context.

Investing a little and often means that you limit your exposure to market fluctuations and therefore you manage risk. Investing aggressively when a special opportunity arises, such as in the Harley Davidson example, makes sense, so the more you take advantage of a situation like that, the more your returns are likely to be if you get it right. So, in summary, invest a little and often, and invest heavily rarely and intelligently. Taking both approaches is most likely to provide you with the best returns overall and in the long run.

In order to maximise your chances of making money, you should aim to get what you don't pay for. That is, pay less for the share than the intrinsic value of it. Sooner or later, the rest of the world will catch up with your thinking. We will explore how you do this in more detail now.

CHAPTER 8:

The share price – get what you don't pay for

'Based on my own personal experience – both as an investor in recent years and an expert witness in years past – rarely do more than three or four variables really count. Everything else is noise.'

Marty Whitman – American investor adviser

DOES YOUR SHOPPING BILL SURPRISE YOU?

By this point the assumption is made that you know who you are and what your likely emotional and psychological behaviours are likely to be under stress and in relation to characteristics such as patience and commitment. It is also assumed that you are willing to invest some time and energy into looking into a particular company, reading as much as you can about the business you are considering and conducting as much independent research as you can.

It is also assumed that you are starting to formulate your own set of rules to which you will consistently adhere when shopping for shares, and that you appreciate that with ownership of shares comes a responsibility as an owner. This is not about buying and selling, it is about investing, and you will need to stick to your plan to achieve its objectives. If you find when grocery shopping that the end bill is always widely adrift of your expectations, you should think long and hard before proceeding further.

However, if you feel that, having read to this stage, you are ready to commit to your own set of consistent investing principles, and you are open to a continual learning process having noted some of the behavioural signposts alluded to thus far, then let us proceed. We will look at some of the measures that have served me well and which are offered purely as some, not all, of a basket of measures that you may wish to consider when assessing whether or not to invest in a particular company.

KEEP IT SIMPLE

I started this chapter with the quote from Marty Whitman because it feels to be true for me from my experience. I have learnt that whilst there is an industry of technical analysis around the stock market, in reality only a relatively small number of measures are worth looking at and these don't require a great deal of academic study to understand or appreciate.

This is a controversial view. After all, many people earn a living from the very activities I am suggesting are of little value to me, so just to be absolutely clear, my experiences and views are offered for you to reflect on, not as recommendations as to how it should be done. This approach worked for me; it may not work for anyone else, but I offer my experience as a means of providing some signposts to the individual who may be new to the world of buying shares and is curious as to how someone else got started. Highly-technical academic books are unlikely to be of much value to you but hopefully this book provides some clarity on how you may choose to begin, and how to go about it before moving onto more academic books if that feels right.

ACCOUNTS ARE NOT FACTS – ACCOUNTANTS CAN TELL THEIR OWN STORIES

The world of accountancy, like the legal world, is filled with professionals who have to adhere to frameworks, or rules if you like, that are imposed on them. Yet the quality and skills of these professionals in interpreting the rules within parameters of legitimacy is what determines their success. Just be aware of the parameters, or to put it simply, the presentation of financial information is not always consistent.

THE GOOD NEWS IS, YOU DON'T NEED TO BE AN ACCOUNTANT UNLESS YOU ARE ONE

Before we proceed, a word of caution. Financial fundamentals, accounting measures, balance sheets and so on, will tell you only part of a story and, in many cases, a story that the company wants you to see. Given that most of us are not forensic accountants, how do we deal with this?

The answer is a rather boring but necessary one. Do your homework. Learn as much as you can about the business, read as much as you can, and patiently assess it. I have never rushed into an investment in my life and this is good advice.

'Anything worth doing is worth doing slowly'.

Mae West – American actress

YOU CAN'T PAY TOMORROW'S BILLS WITH THE MONEY YOU SPENT YESTERDAY

Remember that published accounts are a glimpse into the past, not the future. Like the light from a star that has long gone, it may appear to still be burning brightly, but remember that sometimes it only seems that way. Consider, reflect and keep learning. You will never know everything about a business, but you should try to see it from the inside out as well as the outside in. Be wary of taking only a cursory face value view of the basic financial statistics. After all, would you marry someone based on their vital statistics? If you answered 'Yes', then well done for honesty, but investing may not be your thing.

Always question things, especially if they look good.

> *'Believe those who are seeking the truth. Doubt those who find it.'*
>
> Andre Gide – French author

The better something looks, the more you should question it.

YOU HAVE TO SEE THE BIGGER PICTURE

The final point I wish to make is perhaps the most important. Although I am going to walk through some very simple measures that should interest the potential investor, none of them should be viewed in isolation. A share price in isolation can be relatively meaningless. Even when measures are placed within the context of several others, they can still be relatively meaningless. What is required is a comprehensive helicopter view of a basket of measures combined with additional intelligence from which an informed assessment of a company can be made. The following sections of this book should always be viewed within that context, without exception.

ACCEPT THAT YOU CANNOT KNOW ALL THE DETAILS, SO FOCUS ON WHAT IS IMPORTANT TO YOU

It is also worth noting that from my experience no matter how much research you do, you will always be dealing with making a decision in the context of only some of the information you would ideally like to have. You will often be dealing with imperfect information, but that is the way of the world and you can't avoid it. If you could avoid this, then making perfect decisions consistently would be a lot easier. My view is that you make a decision based on 90% of the picture; the remaining 10% – well that is down to your judgement.

THE SHARE PRICE

> *'There is a tide in the affairs of men which, taken at the flood, leads on to fortune.'*
>
> William Shakespeare – English playwright

THE PLACE TO START IS THE SHARE PRICE. HOW MUCH WILL IT COST YOU TO BUY PART OF A BUSINESS?

So let's start with an obvious one. The share price. Where the share price is concerned, the objective is actually to get what you are not paying for. In other words, to buy a great company for a good, or bargain, price. However, in most cases, people do not get what they pay for in that they often pay over the odds as a share price is at its peak, and often sell at a lower price when the share is heading south at an alarming rate. That is how to destroy wealth and is the opposite of what we are trying to achieve.

In buying high and selling low, most people become poorer than they were when they started.

Seems like an obvious pattern of behaviour to avoid doesn't it? So very obvious. So few people can actually do it. Most people will roll their eyes and tut at such an obvious pattern of behaviour to avoid, and yet it is only the precious view who can consistently avoid doing this very thing. The reason is equally obvious. Most people do not really understand themselves and their ability to behave in a certain way in certain specific conditions. In short, they are prone to panic and overly influenced by the behaviour of others.

Most people pay over the real intrinsic value of a business when they buy shares because not only have they not researched the business enough, understood it, and been patient in reading as much as they can about it, but also they have been kidding themselves about their own characteristics. Many people would regard an admission that they follow the crowd as a negative thing, so they reflect on themselves with a preferential bias towards behaviours they would ideally like to display, but in reality, don't.

This is of no use to the investor and, in fact, it is very dangerous indeed. There are no right or wrong answers in relation to what kind of personality you are when it comes to investing, there is only the truth. If you can honestly appraise yourself, you will be providing yourself with the advantage you need in your investing career. If you can't, your record in investing is likely to be patchy at best.

COCA COLA AS AN EXAMPLE

So where do we start to think about this a little more intelligently? Let's take a specific example and work it through as a starting point, mindful again that measures such as this are just one small part of a much large picture you will need to assemble before considering investing in a business.

Let's look at the Coca Cola company. The following chart (Figure 3) shows the share price for this company over the past decade starting in 2000 up to 2009. Indications are that in 2010 the price for Coca Cola is edging higher.

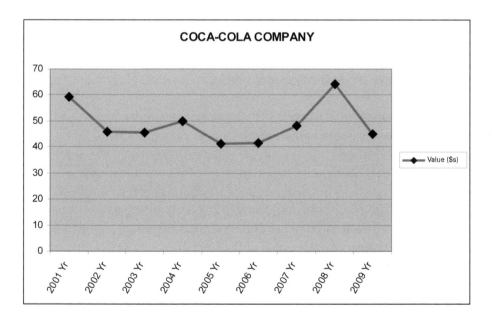

Fig. 3 Share price for Coca Cola company 2000–2009

In 2010 Coca Cola shares have been over $50 a share.

Between 2000 and 2009 the share price of this stock has been somewhat volatile and depending on when you bought into it, you could have been paying what could be considered afterwards as a high or a low price.

For example, the investor buying the stock in 2000 could have paid in excess of $60 a share, whilst the investor in 2003 could have paid around $40 at specific points during that year. It seems to me that as a starting point it is a good idea to try and gauge where the share price of any given stock might be in relation to what I would call its 'normal market price' (in reality there is no such thing). To do this I apply a process I call 'share price averaging', something that has served me very well in estimating the likelihood of whether I am paying too much for a share, based on historical patterns. There is no such thing as a 'normal market price' it is merely a term that I use to describe the price at which, in my judgement, a share is most likely to settle over a period of time on average (not where it will actually be literally).

THERE IS NO GRAVITY IN INVESTING. WHAT GOES UP DOESN'T HAVE TO COME DOWN, AND VICE VERSA

Once again, we remind ourselves that the past is no prediction of the future, but that is not what we are trying to do here. Rather, we are attempting to just get a feel for how relatively expensive the share price is, or is not, today within the context of where it has been. This seems sensible to me and whilst I can hear academic laughter at this concept, it has worked well for me. It is a very simple, overly so, approach, but one that I like because it starts to provide me with a background picture of where the share has been, not where it is going. I will leave complex software tools and pages of technical analysis to minds that must be far superior to mine. Not that I can't understand such approaches, I just don't find it very helpful. I like to keep my approach as simple as possible and I make no apology for it.

HOUSE PRICES ARE A GOOD EXAMPLE

Consider house prices in the UK between 2002 and 2007. In this period they rose dramatically, year on year. If you imagine that trend as a share price on a graph rising sharply year on year, I would suggest that the least risky time to have bought would have been in 2002. In 2007, the probability of paying over the odds for a property would, in my view, have been much higher and therefore would also have been a good time for a seller.

By taking an average price for property in the period measured, and agreeing to pay no more than that average price, the buyer if successful would have secured a property with a reasonable buffer zone against any future fall in house prices. You can call it your margin of error, your safety zone, or whatever you like, but in my view it is prudent to apply this principle to the price you pay for shares in a business.

HAVING A SAFETY MARGIN CAN MANAGE RISK

Having a margin of safety on the price paid for a share has proved to be a very valuable facility in my investing experience. Sometimes the share price may drop slightly from the price you paid for it, but if you already got it for a bargain price and you did your homework correctly, then any loss you incur is more likely to be minimal in comparison with someone who paid significantly over the odds. If the price subsequently drops in that scenario, it may take a very long time indeed to recover the loss. Always build a margin of safety into your investing actions, and life in general.

One way we can do this is by share price averaging over a ten-year period or similar. It is very simple and in isolation can seem quite meaningless in one sense, but it does serve a purpose and I will explain that purpose now.

WHAT USE IS THE AVERAGE PRICE?

The average share price for the Coca Cola company in the period between 2000 and 2009 was broadly around $49. The price at the time of writing is $48.47, so very close to around the average price over the most recent decade. So why even bother working out what the average price is?

'All intelligent investing is value investing – acquiring more that you are paying for. You must value the business in order to value the stock.'

Charlie Munger – Vice Chairman, Berkshire Hathaway

It is all part of working out whether the price you are considering paying is relatively high or low within the context of historical price movements, and in understanding some of the relative risk associated with the price you are paying. This is not about putting a value on a business, which is quite a different matter. It is about estimating the likelihood of paying over the odds in relation to a current share price, although the two do have a relationship, but that is a complex matter we will leave for now.

As a general principle, in looking at the share price alone, assuming you have researched the business sufficiently for your purposes and you have carried out all other analyses you wish to, you should nearly always aim to buy below the average share price for a given stock if possible. However, this principle does not always apply. There are some exceptions such as where there is evidence to suggest that the share price will continue growing and growing, but such examples tend to be the exception, not the norm.

If you take this approach, you will increase the probability of both providing yourself with a buffer zone, or to put it another way, reduce some of the risk whilst at the same time increase the probability of making larger capital gains should the share price go up, and thereby limiting your exposure to potential future losses.

PAY OVER THE ODDS AND THE RISK IS ALL YOURS

Buy a stock that is at or above its average share price and you will stand a larger chance of making a loss, as you will be taking a higher risk with less probability of a buffer zone in the price you are paying, and at the same time you may reduce the margin of any capital gain in the share price that may occur. So if the share price is higher than the average, you should have a really good reason to proceed with purchasing the share. It is a really simple calculation that may seem trivial, but it has worked consistently for me, if only because it has made me pause and reflect and ultimately not buy a company even when I really wanted to. The following quote illustrates this point nicely.

'If you understood a business perfectly and the future of the business, you would need very little in the way of a margin of safety. So, the more vulnerable the business is, assuming you still want to invest in it, the larger margin of safety you'd need. If you're driving a truck across a bridge that says it holds 10,000 pounds and you've got a 9,800 pound vehicle, if the bridge is 6 inches above the crevice it covers, you may feel okay, but if it's over the Grand Canyon, you may feel you want a little larger margin of safety . . .'

1997 Berkshire Hathaway Annual Meeting

The relative importance of buying below the average share price for a stock is largely determined by the size and nature of the business. If you are thinking of buying a small, obscure and relatively high-risk business, you would be wise to maximise your margin of safety. If on the other hand, you are buying a company like Coca Cola (of which there are not many, I might add), whilst I would always advocate waiting until the price is significantly below the average for reasons already outlined, your investment is nevertheless far less risky, given the scope and scale of the business.

'The individual investor should act consistently as an investor and not as a speculator. This means . . . that he should be able to justify every purchase he makes and each price he pays by impersonal, objective reasoning that satisfies him that he is getting more than his money's worth for his purchase.'

Benjamin Graham – American economist

That said, patience and timing are once again your main ally. Warren Buffet bought into Coca Cola when its share price was at one of its lowest points, well below the average, and still holds the stock to this day.

'All there is to investing is picking good stocks at good times and staying with them as long as they remain good companies.'

Warren Buffet – investor

THE PE RATIO – WHAT IT MEANS, WHY IT IS USEFUL AND HOW YOU CAN APPLY IT

There is also a ratio called the 'price to earnings' ratio (PE ratio) which is a simple measure of the price paid for a share relative to the annual net income or profit made by a company.

The main value in using a measure like this is that it enables you to compare various companies on a like-for-like measure. Measures such as the price to earnings ratio amongst others are easily accessible via most online share dealing services and stockbrokers.

Broadly speaking, and this is an arguable point, as are most where investing is concerned, a PE (price to earnings) ratio of 10 or less may indicate that shares in the business are currently trading cheaply. However, as stated, taken in isolation this measure is of little value. It is purely indicative. That said, if you are looking for a bargain, a PE ratio of less than 10 *might* be a good place to start, but it might also indicate something else. That is why nothing should be taken in isolation. Financial measures cannot be used in isolation of a range of others, for the same reason that a medical expert would not assume from someone saying that they have a headache that it must be a brain tumour, the neurotic's favourite.

The more you learn, and the more measures you consider, the less risk you are taking. The share price and the PE ratio are good measures to consider as previously described. A PE ratio of over 20 combined with a share price that is at its highest point in the history of the company for no apparent reason does not scream 'value' to me. The share price and the PE ratio are good initial indicators to consider. Like fish and chips, they go well together.

CHAPTER 9:

Risky business

*'A controversy prevailed among the beasts of the field
as to which of the animals deserved the most credit for
producing the greatest number of whelps at a birth.
They rushed clamorously into the presence of the Lioness
and demanded of her the settlement of the dispute. 'And
you,' they said, 'how many sons have you at a birth?'
The Lioness laughed at them, and said, 'Why! I have only
one; but that one is altogether a thoroughbred Lion.'*

Aesop fable

I don't intend to write too much about risk as a standalone concept.
Some people have made careers out of it, producing elaborate
methodologies, tools and strategies to manage it and mitigate your
exposure to it. Some of it may be of some value, but most of it is
technical nonsense.

The reality is that you don't need to be an expert in risk management,
or have studied it academically to a high level, or have any other
special pre-requisite skill to avoid being exposed to high risk. Just aim
to buy a thoroughbred lion. I don't mean that literally, of course. That
would probably be considered a very high risk.

SOME EXAMPLES OF LOW-RISK COMPANIES

Examples of companies I would currently consider to be in this
category are businesses like Tesco or Coca Cola. Both of these
companies have a combination of business strengths, brand loyalty,
financial power, strong committed management and so on that
provide them with a massive competitive advantage that is likely to

be sustainable for the medium-term future and beyond. If you buy into companies that have qualities like these, your exposure to making significant losses is a lot less than in smaller, higher-risk ventures.

But with low risk comes low reward, right? Well yes and no. There is a famous quote about investing in large companies that goes like this:

'Elephants don't gallop.'

Jim Slater – investor

Whilst I understand where Jim Slater was coming from, I do not entirely agree. Find yourself in the wilderness and faced with an angry charging bull elephant and you may find that whilst they can't exactly gallop, they really can shift faster than you would want them to. I believe in diversifying your investments in both large and small companies. If you have done your homework to a sufficient level, a hybrid approach to investing will serve you well.

'Risk comes from not knowing what you're doing.'

Warren Buffett – investor

As alluded to earlier, there is no substitute for hard work, research and then more research. I stress once again that this does not require an academic qualification or knowledge and experience of business, just the ability to read and to think critically about what it is that you have read, and to make sense of it in a way that is relevant to you.

You might think on reading Buffet's quote that you are somehow not qualified to be buying shares and that therefore it is 'high risk'. I would suggest you are wrong and you have misunderstood what Warren Buffet is getting at. Mr Buffet started investing when he was very young and relatively inexperienced, yet what he had was the right attitude and commitment to an approach that consistently worked for him. The Buffet investment ethic is a sound one. So, do your homework and investigate and understand your considered investments, and you will not need to lose sleep over ways of calculating risk that may not help you at all.

BE REALISTIC AND YOU WILL AVOID DISAPPOINTMENT

You should be realistic about your goals.

'In this business if you're good, you're right six times out of ten. You're never going to be right nine times out of ten.'

Peter Lynch – Wall Street investor

Expect some of your shares to go down, and some to go up. The more you do your research and the more you learn over time, the relative proportion of the latter in relation to the former should increase. If it does not, you may want to step back and reflect on what might be going wrong.

'It's not whether you're right or wrong that's important, but how much money you make when you're right and how much you lose when you're wrong.'

George Soros – American currency speculator

A tolerance for ambiguity will serve you well as an investor, as will an inquiring mind.

RISK RATINGS

Most online stockbrokers and share dealing services provide a risk rating, or risk score, for a given share. These of course change quickly, with a classic example being banks. Prior to 2006, banks were largely given a very low-risk score, meaning that they were deemed to be very safe. During 2008, I witnessed some banks who had previously had a risk rating of around 250 zoom to a risk score of in excess of 1,000 in a very short period of time. If this had happened to you, what should you do as a consistent investor? Do you think that Warren Buffet would have stuck to his 'hold forever' position in these circumstances?

If you do, you have not understood a key part of the first part of this book properly. Buffet does sell shares, contrary to popular myth, as do I, as noted in my Barclays example; it is just that for me, it is exceptional behaviour, not the norm.

It is about exercising your own judgement and understanding that sometimes you will be wrong, or you can be right but the rest of the world goes wrong, and it can happen quickly. Remaining calm and sticking to your plan is generally a good idea, but if the ship is sinking, then your planned destination may no longer be an option. So you need to modify your plan, but always understand rationally why you are doing what you are doing, and never sell irrationally. In this way you will maximise your defences against irrational actions that can be costly and which present the typical investor with the most frequent realisation of their exposure to risk; or to put it another way, selling at a loss.

AN EXAMPLE OF MANAGING RISK – BARCLAYS

I sold Barclays shares as they were heading down, and I sold them for a reasonable price and a reasonable loss but, unlike most investors, I didn't turn my back on the business. Instead I watched convinced enough that the market was being irrational and that contrary to popular opinion, Barclays would continue as a business and one day bounce back. I then bought back into Barclays and made a significant gain and if I had sold them, profit.

According to the risk ratings at the time and general opinion this was a massive risk and chances were I would lose my money. So why did I do it? Arrogance? No. It was quite a boring reason once again, and not at all anything clever. Just a rational approach. I had spent a lot of time studying the top management of the bank, their behaviour, the strengths and weaknesses of the business and how it was positioning itself in the economic crisis unfolding both around it and to an extent within it. That research gave me confidence that, far from taking a massive risk, I was actually realising an obvious opportunity; it was just heavily disguised and most people could not see through it.

'You're neither right nor wrong because other people agree with you. You're right because your facts are right and your reasoning is right— and that's the only thing that makes you right. And if your facts and reasoning are right, you don't have to worry about anybody else.'

Warren Buffet – investor

Of course you must also guard against thinking it is clever to wade into chaos thinking that it must be a great opportunity. Take calculated risks making sure that you have understood what you feel you need to.

'It is remarkable how much long-term advantage people like us have gotten by trying to be consistently not stupid, instead of trying to be very intelligent.'

Charlie Munger – Vice Chairman, Berkshire Hathaway

DON'T TRY AND BE CLEVER, JUST TRY NOT TO BE STUPID

It is not about being clever, it is more about avoiding stupidity which is often cleverly disguised as a sure-fire exciting new investment opportunity recommended by a 'share tipping' service that just happens to be in the business of selling shares.

'There are known knowns. These are things we know that we know. There are known unknowns. That is to say, there are things we know we don't know.

But, there are also unknown unknowns. These are things we don't know we don't know.'

Donald Rumsfeld – US Secretary of Defense, 2001–2006 (during a Pentagon briefing)

Although it is questionable whether Donald Rumsfeld was actually trying to be clever here, in a way, as far as investing is concerned, he was. Always keep this type of mentality in mind and consider what you think you know in the context of both what you know you don't know and what you might not even know you don't know. If that makes sense, you have been reading this book too long – take a break.

KNOW WHAT YOU ARE PREPARED TO PAY

Work out what you are prepared to buy a stock at and wait to get it at that price, a price which should ideally be below its average historical value. Often a company facing a temporary storm will appear to be high risk, but remember it may only seem to be that way. That does not make it so.

A well-known speaker started off his seminar by holding up a $20 bill. In the room of 200, he asked, 'Who would like this $20 bill?'

Hands started going up.

He said, 'I am going to give this $20 to one of you but first, let me do this.' He proceeded to crumple the dollar bill up.

He then asked, 'Who still wants it?'

Still the hands were up in the air.

'Well,' he replied, 'What if I do this?' And he dropped it on the ground and started to grind it into the floor with his shoe.

He picked it up, now all crumpled and dirty. 'Now who still wants it?' Still the hands went into the air.

'My friends, you have all learned a very valuable lesson. No matter what I did to the money, you still wanted it because it did not decrease in value. It was still worth $20.'

Author unknown

No matter how muddied in the press a company may be, if your research, judgement and more research suggest that everyone else is behaving irrationally, you may be onto an opportunity. Sometimes you will get it right, and sometimes you won't. Get it right six times out of ten, and you should start to accumulate wealth. If you get it wrong nine times out of ten, you should stop what you are doing and become a financial adviser instead.

CHAPTER 10:

Revenue and pretax profit. Are they getting bigger?

'If a man who cannot count finds a four-leaf clover, is he lucky?'

Stanislaw J. Lec – Polish poet

NUMBERS – DON'T' PANIC

Some basic numbers apply here. You don't need to be an accountant to understand the revenue and pre-tax profit figures for a company over a period of time, or worry about business terminology that might seem a bit strange at first. The key point in looking at them is the trend, the pattern in the numbers. Is it up, down, or a bit of both?

More importantly, are any of them negative? I never cease to be amazed at how many people actually buy shares in a company where the pre-tax profit figure is negative, meaning that the company not only failed to make any money, it actually lost it. If you buy shares in a company that is good at losing money, well, guess what is going to happen to your money!

LOOK FOR CONSISTENT GROWTH

All businesses, like people, can have a bad year. The issue is whether it can be explained as a relatively temporary phenomenon that happened for a good reason, or whether it might indicate a trend. As a general principle, I would buy shares only in a company that has consistent positive growth in its revenue/turnover over several years, and the same principle would be applied to the pre-tax profit figures. You can find both easily via almost any online share dealing facility (I use the HSBC Invest-direct service which is superb; see website www. hsbc.co.uk) and having targeted a stock, just click on the fundamentals tab and scroll down and you will usually find the revenue/turnover figures for the company over several years, and the same for the pre-tax profit. You can also find this information, and a lot more, from the company website by looking at the financial reports and statements.

The reason I stated that as a general principle this is the case, is that there is one scenario that might be an exception and that is where the drop in the growth in the figures, or even the loss, is a one-off, a passing storm, something

'The important thing is not to stop questioning.'

Albert Einstein – scientist

that is unlikely to be repeated. For example, if a company reports that year 1 pre-tax profit was £1 million, year 2 was £3.5 million, year 3 was £2 million, year 4 was £ 4.5 million and year 5 was £6 million, there may have been a one-off reasonable explanation as to what happened in year 3. It is your job, and responsibility as a consistent investor, to investigate and stop looking into the business only when you are satisfied that you have answered your questions.

GREAT COMPANIES GROW

A great company will grow. It will have a superior business strategy that is aligned with committed management who have the right skills, attitude and owner orientation to take the business forward. This will deliver growth to the business that is consistent and sustainable and in turn at some point the market will notice and the share price will go up. As you may be starting to guess by this point, if you have done your homework, worked out the value of a business to you in terms of the price you are prepared to pay for it, and taken all of the steps you can reasonably take to assess the business to your satisfaction, you just may get to buy the stock at the point before the market realises that it is undervalued.

'Most people get interested in stocks when everyone else is. The time to get interested is when no on else is. You can't buy what is popular and do well'.

Warren Buffet – investor

Just remember that investing is rarely exciting. In fact it shouldn't be. It should be boring. Excitement can be your enemy, cloud your judgement and lead to a fallible and sub-optimum investment decision. Some of the best investment decisions you are likely to make should bore your friends senseless. If your friends find your investments interesting, that may be a bad thing.

HOW YOU SPEND YOUR MONEY SAYS A LOT ABOUT YOU

Something worth considering when looking at a potential investment is how the business spends its money, and how much of it is spent, and what the return is on the money it spends. We all know someone who appears to spend money as if it is going out of fashion. Would you invest in them? The consistent investor should look to identify businesses that behave like squirrels, and these squirrels should want to take over the forest. Grey squirrels would make great investors. Red squirrels should give up on squirrelling.

CHAPTER 11:

Is the company making a lot of money from the money it spends or spending a lot of the money it makes?

'Not everything that counts can be counted, and not everything that can be counted counts.'

Sign that hung in Albert Einstein's office at Princeton

GETTING BACK MORE THAN YOU PUT IN

The return on the capital employed explained

Put simply, there is a ratio that measures this. You will see it on the front summary page of a given company using most online stock-broker services or investment facilities and it will be called ROCE, which stands for Return on the Capital Employed.

Put simply, this measure shows the return that a business gets for its assets or how much it is losing due to its liabilities. The more positive this figure is, the better; the smaller, or even negative this figure is, the worse. I have never invested in a business with a negative ROCE figure, and never will. To me, it is a measure of safety in the business. I like the business to have a big profit margin and relatively small exposure to liabilities. That is not a recommendation as to how you should invest, just my personal bias.

No company can, in the long run, sustain a negative ROCE. Oddly, like companies that report a recurring negative pre-tax profit figure, these measures do not stop some people from buying shares in such companies. To me, this is no different from having an operation from a surgeon who has never operated before. If you invest your money in a business that has never made any money, what do you seriously think is going to happen to your money? Remember, a positive ROCE figure is a good thing. Anything less than positive is a serious warning sign that, in my subjective and arguable opinion, requires significant further investigation if you are considering investing.

> '*In the short run, the market is a voting machine, but in the long run it is a weighing machine.*'
>
> Ben Graham – American economist

One again this is purely my personal preference and indicative of the kind of sectors I invest in where a negative ROCE figure is less common; but nevertheless, it is an approach I advocate. A healthy ROCE ratio is indicative of a business that is adding value, and therefore creating wealth through its activities and existence.

As with any aspect of investing, it is recommended that you take the time to look into what measures such as the ROCE actually mean so you are clear that you have your own understanding of what it means to you, and to learn as much as you can about all of the other measures that are worth noting. Speaking of which, let's look at a potentially really important one next: shares that pay dividends.

CHAPTER 12:

Consistent investing can pay dividends

'A lot of people love Oreos. So their manufacturer is making money. That means more dividends for shareholders.'

Maria Bartiromo – American business news anchor

WHAT IS A DIVIDEND?

Dividends are payments made to shareholders by a business, and I like investments that pay dividends. As a shareholder in a business that pays a dividend you will receive a cash payment (usually) in proportion to the number of shares you own. I really like this idea. Let me explain why.

Owning a share means that you own part of a business. A real business, employing real people, doing real things. Think about that.

If you see owning shares as owning the business, which is what it is, then you are proactively, not passively, part of that business. You have invested in it. You are taking a share in the risk. Risk should carry a reward, and here is where dividends really become important.

'I rarely think the market is right. I believe non dividend stocks aren't much more than baseball cards. They are worth what you can convince someone to pay for it.'

Mark Cuban – American billionaire

In an ideal situation you will buy a share in a business which is undervalued, and over time the share will increase in value to the point at which you are very pleased with the capital gain you have seen in the share price. Then guess what, you also receive a cash bonus in the form of a dividend payment! Sounds like a great concept to me. But what if it doesn't work out quite like that?

DIVIDENDS CAN HELP TO MITIGATE RISK

Let's say that the stock stays the same or, even worse, actually goes down a little in the short term. If you have invested in a business that does not pay any dividends, you have no compensation for what has happened, just less money than you had when you invested. However, if the business pays dividends and continues to honour that commitment (in the same way that companies like Coca Cola have historically done) then it mitigates some of your risk. Or to put it another way, you still get some income from the investment which could be seen to offset your loss in the share price, should that have happened.

As a general principle I tend to invest only in businesses that have a sustained track record of paying dividends. However, there are some important points to consider in relation to dividends.

'When buying a dividend stock, the quality of the company is the number one consideration. Given enough time, a quality company will always rise above lesser competition. When your holding period is forever, it is inevitable that a superior stock will eventually out-perform second-tier players.'

Warren Buffet – investor

QUALITY MATTERS

The quality of the company is everything. Large quality companies like Coca Cola and Royal Dutch Shell 'A' shares are relatively low-risk investments, generally speaking, and yet they pay a reasonable interest on your investment in the form of dividends.

Royal Dutch Shell 'A' shares also pay a good dividend. That is besides any capital gain in the share price you may have benefited from by buying the share price at a lower price than the current one. Let's talk a bit about what dividend yield is.

DIVIDEND YIELD – HOW MUCH MONEY YOU WILL GET BACK?

In my view, dividend yield is the only dividend calculation you need to bother with. You will see others if you look into it such as dividend cover and payout ratios and all manner of equations and measures. The more you learn about investing and the various ratios and measures people use, the more you will learn about the sheer scale of different techniques and measures that exist that run the whole range from quite logical and useful to completely barmy. Stick with dividend yield for starters and if you really do have a desire to learn about all of the other measures, then great, go for it; it certainly won't harm your investing capability. However, I have been there and done that; I have found what is comfortable and works for me.

You can work out the dividend yield very, very easily. Simply take the current share price, take the current dividend per share, and divide the current dividend per share price by the current share price, and multiply it by 100 to give you the percentage dividend yield.

Take this example.

Company A has a share price of £1 and pays a 10p dividend per share. So you take the 10p, divide it by £1 (so 100p) then multiply it by 100 and, hey presto, the dividend yield for this share is 10%. If you find a solid business that pays 10%, tell me.

CAUTION – IF IT LOOKS TOO GOOD TO BE TRUE, IT IS

Now a word of warning. There are some really good companies who can normally sustain paying a dividend yield of around 5–6–7%. If you find a company paying anything higher than around 8–10% you should exercise caution, because in many cases it will either not be sustainable or not in the long-term interests of the business or the shareholder, or both, to do so.

Indeed there are many who would argue that it is not in the interest of a business at all to pay any dividends which may then restrict the ability of the company to re-invest to the level it would like with a view to growing faster and further. Under certain circumstances there are occasions when not paying a dividend is very justified, such as when doing so might jeopardise the future sustainability of the business. However, such instances tend to happen to the wrong kind of businesses anyway that find themselves in a bad position due to inept management, leadership or business strategy, or any combination of those. Coca Cola has paid uninterrupted dividend payments to its shareholders since around 1920.

> '*Do you know the only thing that gives me pleasure? It's to see my dividends coming in.*'
>
> John D. Rockefeller – American industrialist

DON'T BE GREEDY

The trick is to get the highest dividend yield you can from a quality company. Much of that is achieved by paying a good price for the share in the first place. Sometimes you can get a high dividend yield if you can wait and wait for a quality company that pays dividends to suffer a temporary storm, and then buy the dividend-paying stock at an unusually low price providing you with a greater yield per share.

Your dividend yield under such circumstances can be much higher because the share price has gone down but the dividend has not (at least, not yet!) so the yield is far more. To take the previous example, what is the dividend yield if company A shares have now fallen to 50p (but you are as confident as you can be that this is irrational and the business is still fundamentally sound) but is still paying a 10p per share dividend? I am hoping you have already calculated what I am about to write next.

If you worked out that Company A is now paying a dividend yield of 20%, well done. If your answer was two hours and thirty six minutes, go back to chapter 1.

> *'There are really only three kinds of people in the world: those who can count and those who can't.'*

Warren Buffet – investor

DON'T FOLLOW THE FASHION

So let's say you did well, found a company like BP and bought it when it was out of fashion (*everyone thought we were going to be driving bio-diesel solar powered cars next year but it turned out it might take a little bit longer*) and the share price has since recovered leaving you with a nice gain in the value of your asset and you are also now getting a dividend yield of at least 7% on your investment, paid in regular instalments. What do you do with the money after your tax has been paid?

What you don't do is withdraw it from your account and spend it. You could do that, but in my view that would be stupid.

> *'Two things are infinite: the universe and human stupidity; and I'm not sure about the universe.'*

Albert Einstein – scientist

MONEY CAN SNOWBALL

It would be stupid because you can use dividend payments over time to start to accrue your wealth. Over time, this can create a snowball effect as your wealth compounds. Imagine getting to the point at which your dividend payments alone are becoming enough to make it worthwhile re-investing them alone, aside from anything you can top it up with yourself. When you get to that stage, and I hope you do, you will be on the verge of creating a self-sustaining money engine. It is what is meant by the old phrase 'money makes money'. In fact, it does.

Getting your money to work for you is indeed quite possible if you adopt some of the core principles discussed so far and apply them consistently and patiently over time. The more time, the more money. I have a 120-year plan (not endorsed by my wife) that would ensure that my grandchildren grow into very wealthy people indeed. Investing is a relay marathon, not a sprint.

CHAPTER 13:

Buy companies that can live within their means

'A bank is a place where they lend you an umbrella in fair weather and ask for it back when it begins to rain.'

Robert Frost – American poet

You may have to change and take some tough decisions. Like you, companies should live below their means.

I have always thought that if you need to borrow money you can't afford it. I take the same approach with investing. I consistently try to target businesses that have a relatively low level of gearing (debt). Why?

DEBT IS BAD

A brief explanation of why

Well, in short, having debt is a bad idea for so many reasons, not least of which is that it makes you, or a business, vulnerable. Some debts are largely unavoidable for most of us, such as a mortgage, but I will let you conduct your own research into how much debt the average person is now servicing, and that is besides the billions of deficit the UK Government looks set to run up. This is all very bad indeed. Much of the world is running on the basis that all of this debt can and will be repaid. We have in 2008 and 2009 and beyond lived through a significant economic shock caused by the collapse of the sub-prime lending market in the first instance. Let's reflect on that for a moment.

Debt is a form of imprisonment
Debt is to our economy what heroin is to the drug addict. It provides a temporary fix and some apparently pleasurable short-term benefits, but the price that is paid over the longer term can be catastrophic. It requires ever-increasing amounts in order to maintain its record and, of course, that is not sustainable and ends in tragedy. The best way to grow is by creating wealth, not debt.

> *'A billion here, a billion there, and pretty soon you're talking about real money.'*
>
> Everett Dirksen – US Congressman

Financial institutions, who should know all about money and investing, started to slowly relax the rules by which they allowed people to borrow money. Instead of adhering to long-established and consistently-applied methodologies in the distribution of loans, money was flowing freely, too freely. At around the same time, complex new financial instruments started to emerge that were re-packaging debts and selling them on for ever-increasing profits: structured finance springs to mind. All of this was sold very slickly to people who should have known better, and in fact, did know better. So what happened?

It takes a brave person to stand alone
Everyone was happy as anyone could borrow money, banks were selling on the debts for massive amounts of more money, and few people were really stopping to pause or reflect on the near hysteria that had engulfed the banking world.

As everyone seemed to be doing well, the facade of the system held up and it was intoxicating for the majority who got swept up in it, including some really clever people. People were, by and large, following the crowd, as were banks. As one financial institution saw that another had increased its profits massively through sub-prime lending, it felt compelled to do so as well or it would seem as though it was underperforming and, as a manager in that bank, you would possibly lose your job. Self preservation is human nature, and in that kind of context it can lead to disaster, as indeed it most certainly did.

I didn't get caught up in that mindset. Not because I have any gift of foresight or particular talent at investing. I just stuck to my consistent set of principles regarding investing. It really was as simple as that. Not that I emerged unscathed completely as, at one point during late 2008, my portfolio had reduced in value by around 35% in total, although given what was happening in the world, that was actually quite a good performance. Today, I am around 75% up on where I was in 2008. The past year has been the best for me in over a decade, just by applying the principles in this book (and wider knowledge I have gained over the years, largely by reading a lot which I can't recommend enough).

Shares were over-heating and priced above their value, in some cases I sold. I then waited for the inevitable bursting of what was obviously a significant bubble. When that happened and the price of shares came down significantly, I started to buy shares in larger quantities than I had done in years. I am still doing that at the time of writing, although month by month now it is starting to get harder to find quality great businesses where the share price is still low enough to get them at a price that I consider to be a bargain. But they are still out there for the patient and persistent investor.

The less debt you have, the more freedom you have
So debt, shockingly-poor financial management by banks, and human behaviour in following the crowd got the world into its current financial mess, from which it will emerge damaged and the recovery will be slow and painful. Part of the problem was caused by the well known phrase 'the credit crunch' when banks went from one extreme to the other in terms of lending money. Now if you think about it, if you had very little debt as a business, this economic hurricane that was

taking place around you and causing your competitors to go bump would have had little impact on you. If you owe only a little amount of money in relation to your cash flow and cash in the bank, so what if lines of credit dry up? (Assuming of course that your customers stay in business!)

Many businesses, too many, were not in that position and had taken on far too much debt to fund overly-aggressive expansion in many cases. Once again, obvious, stupid mistakes. Businesses were living way beyond their means in many cases.

> *'I'm living so far beyond my income that we may almost be said to be living apart.'*
>
> E. E. Cummings – American poet

I don't intend to dwell on the real complexities of what has happened in the latest recession, that is perhaps something for a different book or someone else to write about, but these things really are quite foreseeable if you just practise certain investing principles consistently. I am already wondering what will cause the next economic shock or growth bubble. Will it be the end of cheap oil (yes, it is cheap now!) around 2015, give or take a few years, that causes the next recession or economic meltdown? Or perhaps it will be caused by an economic bubble in newly-emergent industries relating to sustainable energy or similar.

> *'Stock market bubbles don't grow out of thin air. They have a solid basis in reality, but reality as distorted by a misconception.'*
>
> George Soros – currency speculator

LIFE WILL ALWAYS SURPRISE YOU NO MATTER HOW CLEVER YOU THINK YOU ARE, BUT BEING AWARE OF THAT HELPS

In reality, it will probably be neither and will turn out to be a surprise; but whatever it is, I am unlikely to be up to my eyeballs in debt when it happens and neither will I have put all of my money into an oil company, or a solar panel manufacturer. The point I am making is once again about risk. If you know how to manage risk, investing in the stock market is not half as 'risky' as some would have you believe.

HOW MUCH DEBT IS MANAGEABLE?

Debt is a very bad thing in large doses; in small and manageable quantities it is a part of life in the 21st century. So how do we know if a business has dangerously high levels of debt?

'If you think nobody cares if you're alive, try missing a couple of car payments.'

Earl Wilson – US politician

GEARING, OTHERWISE KNOWN AS DEBT

It's time for exploring another measure and this one is called the 'gearing ratio'. There are several similar ratios that can be equally useful including something like total debt divided by total equity, or an equity ratio (equity divided by assets), or a debt ratio such as total debt divided by total assets. If any of this sounds confusing, don't worry about it. Online stock brokers and share dealing services provide a wealth of intelligence and data about a business, and having familiarised yourself with how your particular share dealing provider shows this information, you will quickly locate the net gearing ratio already calculated towards the bottom of the financial fundamentals. Just make sure you understand a little about how it has been calculated.

As a principle I tend to discount any business that has an excessively high level of gearing, which for me is a net gearing figure of above 35%. That is not to say that I always discount a business if the figure was higher, just that there would have to be an especially strong reason for continuing to evaluate the potential investment were the figure to be above my personal preferred threshold.

THE MORE DEBT YOU TAKE ON, THE HIGHER THE RISK

The higher the net gearing figure, the riskier the investment becomes. This is basically because debt has to paid back no matter what happens to your sales. Costs are generally more fixed, whilst income for most businesses is variable and can fluctuate wildly. The manufacturer of high-end electronic consumer goods that is very heavily geared is likely to face a potentially serious problem in the event of a sudden economic downturn. The debt, however, as a fixed cost, would remain. This is how large numbers of businesses go under.

A business in the same sector with little or no debt and a healthy bank balance is far more likely to weather the economic storm. Recessions are nothing new, they have happened before and will do so again. Does any business really have an excuse for not being prepared for them?

'Technically, the crash of 1987 bears an uncanny resemblance to the crash of 1929. The shape and extent of the decline and even the day-to-day movements of stock prices track very closely.'

George Soros in *The Alchemy of Finance*

BE PREPARED TO WEATHER A STORM

So the world will almost certainly face further financial shocks and economic events that will surprise us, and whilst we can't say when it will happen or how exactly it will play out next time around, as George Soros has indicated, sometimes it really can feel like a little bit of history repeating as the stock market will continue to behave in both a rational and irrational manner without warning.

'It's only when the tide goes out that you learn who's been swimming naked.'

Warren Buffet – investor

That is why it is so important to think about the business, and not the share price or even what the market is really doing at all.

RECESSION, LIKE VOLATILITY, IS NOT ALL BAD

Recessions sort out capable businesses that are well managed and really creating wealth from those which have just been riding a wave in buoyant times. Many substandard businesses can be profitable in times of prosperity, but how many could survive in times of austerity?

Buying into a great business is always the way to go. The stock market is just your door into it. Choosing when to open it is the key issue but you should not concern yourself with trying to time the market. That is quite pointless. Rather, as explained earlier, find a great company and buy into it for what you believe to be a good and fair price that is ideally below what you consider the real value of the company to be. A great business will continue to grow, be profitable, behave responsibly and increase in value.

CHAPTER 14:

A great company has quality leadership

'An army of lions commanded by a deer will never be an army of lions.'

Napoleon Bonaparte – French military and political leader

BUSINESSES FAIL BECAUSE PEOPLE FAIL

You should invest only in a great company that is run by great people. A great company run by inadequate managers and leaders will ultimately suffer and possibly fail. There needs to be balance on both measures to seriously consider investing in the business, unless you are adequately prepared to shoulder the implications of not following this principle.

The importance of the quality of the management running a company cannot be over-estimated. The future success of a business depends on this and the quality of the business strategies that these people deploy. The return on your investment also depends on this.

'In financing growing companies, we always looked for human value that didn't appear on the balance sheet, the quality of management, especially its entrepreneurial drive.'

Michael Milken – American financier

WOULD YOU INVEST IN THESE PEOPLE?

If you don't know if you would invest in the people running a particular company that you are considering buying shares in, then you don't know enough about the company to proceed. Is there evidence that the management can manage risk and do they provide a vision for the business that is clearly articulated? How have they performed in their role based on the measures of your choice, not theirs, over time? Have they made what have subsequently turned out to be bad decisions and what is the organisational culture for addressing that within the business?

One thing you should really be wary of is when a company that is not doing that well starts to try to justify it with a slickly-written load of nonsense in the company reports. Look closely at the actual words used by the Chairman and the Chief Executive Officer, for they can mask a multitude of sins.

'Of one thing be certain: if a CEO is enthused about a particularly foolish acquisition, both his internal staff and his outside advisors will come up with whatever projections are needed to justify his stance. Only in fairy tales are emperors told that they are naked.'

Warren Buffet – investor

LEARN FROM EXPERIENCE

I have read, and continue to read, a lot of company annual reports and market updates of various kinds. After you have read enough of them (back to front, as the stuff they don't really expect you to read is always at the back), you start to get a feel for them as you do with people as you age. The older you get, hopefully, the wiser.

One thing I have always found slightly odd with Western culture, be it the EU or the United States, is our attitude towards older people. Before you think I am losing the plot here and ask what this has to do with investing, consider the following. In the Far East, as a person becomes older, their wisdom in many cultures gains additional weight; in effect, there is a sort of kudos that comes with being what is considered to be older. In the West, we seem to do the reverse, and often the elderly in our society appear to feel largely redundant.

We also, in my view, patronise our elderly population, belittle their capabilities and infantilise them. We seem to have forgotten that, in many cases, this is a group of people who may have experienced a world war and returned to tell the tale with not a minute to reflect and no post-traumatic counselling. They have seen poverty the likes of which many in the younger generation will have no concept, and seen several recessions, governments, and countless fashions and fads have their five minutes of fame before the next one arrives.

Believe me, we should listen to older people, for they have accrued more knowledge and experience, and that has value for those with open ears, hearts and minds. The same principle applies to investing: there is no limit on my capacity to learn from those with greater experience and knowledge, and this approach will serve you well.

'Only one who devotes himself to a cause with his whole strength and soul can be a true master. For this reason mastery demands all of a person.'

Albert Einstein – scientist

Target the very best people in what you are interested in and learn as much as you can about their behaviour, strategy and what worked for them and why, and reflect on it. Whatever you do, do not think you can do the same. Different approaches work for different people in different ways at different points in history.

Many investors have tried to imitate the value investing techniques that they perceive the likes of Warren Buffet to deploy, but become frustrated at their comparative lack of success. An approach such as this is akin to paying to see a concert and having a tribute act perform. Nobody else is Warren Buffet, and he has been investing for a very long time with a particular set of personal characteristics and an approach that worked for him at specific points in our history. They may not work again in the same way, even for him, and he knows that. Many people new to investing do not seem to have understood how the same moves don't work if the rules of the game have changed. That said, learn about what makes great managers great, and use those measures to assess the relative quality of the people running the business you have targeted.

'A lot of companies have chosen to downsize, and maybe that was the right thing for them. We chose a different path. Our belief was that if we kept putting great products in front of customers, they would continue to open their wallets.'

Steve Jobs – CEO, Apple

Does the top management give you confidence that the business will not only be there in ten years' time, but will have consistently grown? Is the evidence on how this is likely to be achieved clear? These are important questions. Some management teams have a very clear sense of their direction of travel and how they are going to get there.

DOES THE MANAGEMENT HAVE THE OWNER'S EYE?

Is there evidence that the management are acting in the interest of shareholders and are committed to adding value to the business, or are they paying themselves rewards that are disproportionate to the performance of the business, whilst not taking a stake in it themselves?

'Good leaders must first become good servants.'

Robert Greenleaf – Founder Servant, Leadership Movement

IF YOU OWN A SHARE OF A BUSINESS, YOU ARE PART OWNER OF THAT BUSINESS AND ALL OF ITS STAFF WORK FOR YOU

Remember that as a shareholder in the business, you are a part owner of that business, and everyone in it therefore works for you. If it doesn't seem that way, you should reflect on why this is the case. I personally like management teams that have a large percentage of their wealth tied up in the business, as long as it is not so large that they wield unchecked power. You should exercise caution in management teams who can be reckless with your money without any consequence on their wealth also.

'The leader follows in front.'
Unknown

I value frank and honest accounts of the performance of a business and I am wary of companies which hide behind marketing spin and nonsense. A company should report both its successes and failures with equal fanfare. Any good business relationship has to be based on trust that both parties are being open with each other, therefore sincerity and integrity are important. In fact those characteristics in leaders are critical. Many of the company reports that I read fall far short of my benchmark for this and I continue to watch them with a curiosity to see how they will perform over time.

'Organization doesn't really accomplish anything. Plans don't accomplish anything, either. Theories of management don't much matter. Endeavours succeed or fail because of the people involved. Only by attracting the best people will you accomplish great deeds.'
Colin Powell – American Statesman

PAY ATTENTION TO EXCUSES

Some of the smartest investors in and leaders of the best companies I have ever seen have a modesty in their persona and a humble attitude to their achievements. This approach is far more likely to warrant further investigation than the management team that attempts to explain away unsatisfactory performance on external factors and a range of other excuses.

During 2008 and 2009, I observed a number of businesses that hit hard times and blamed the recession. In many cases, this was blatantly not true, the UK high street retailer Woolworths being a good example of a business that had been dead on its feet for years and the demise of which was, in my view, very little to do with the global economy and far more to do with its management. Integrity matters. Look for opportunities where you have a high level of confidence in the values of the people running the business – it will serve you well.

Another characteristic that will serve you well is the ability to spread your investment over a number of great and different companies in a number of different sectors. It is all about eggs and baskets.

CHAPTER 15:

Don't just buy eggs, and have more than one basket

DIVERSIFICATION HELPS TO MANAGE THAT 'RISK' WORD AGAIN

Where investing in shares is concerned you will hear the word 'diversification' a lot, and it can mean different things to different people. Let's start with a very simple definition, and then let's keep it as simple as possible without making it simpler than it should be.

A definition:

'The act or practice of manufacturing a variety of products, investing in a variety of securities, selling a variety of merchandise, etc., so that a failure in or an economic slump affecting one of them will not be disastrous.'

Definition of diversification (www.dictionary.com)

This is not a bad definition at all in my view. You may be familiar with the old saying, 'don't put all of your eggs in one basket'. Have you ever really thought that through and what it means?

'My ventures are not in one bottom trusted,
Nor to one place; nor is my whole estate
Upon the fortune of this present year:
Therefore, my merchandise makes me not sad.'

William Shakespeare – English playwright

Some people really don't get the concept of diversification and why it is a good idea, which in my view, it is.

AN EXAMPLE TO ILLUSTRATE THE VALUE OF DIVERSIFICATION

During the late 1990s, many investors seemed to think that diversification was owning say 20 to 30 different stocks. The only problem was that in many cases they were all in the technology sector, and then, when that went bump, diversification did them very little good. The reason for that is that they were not practising diversification in their share purchases, they had just made a very common mistake and far from reducing their exposure to risk, they had massively increased it. The fad for technology shares towards the end of the last decade is a very strong argument in favour of the value of diversification.

Once again, the word 'risk' crops up. It runs throughout everything in investing, as in life. The trick is to learn how to play with it in such a way that you can increase the likelihood of it working to your advantage, rather than against you.

Diversification is also a controversial and widely debated area. Some of the world's most successful investors may take the view that you need to diversify your investments only if you don't know what you are doing. I don't agree with that, but that is just my view. The point is that it is really a case of what works for you, and you are much more likely to find out the less financially painful way, the better briefed and informed you are about what diversification is and what it can mean for you.

Before we get into looking at some specific ways in which managing diversification can help you, I would make the following recommendation. You would be well advised not to have more than 10% of your portfolio wealth invested in any one share, and preferably less than 5%.

Let's consider some ways of looking at how diversification can be applied in helping you to reduce your exposure to risk, and increase the likelihood of profiting from your investing career.

CHAPTER 16:

Does size matter?

'A tree trunk the size of a man grows from a blade as thin as a hair. A tower nine stories high is built from a small heap of earth.'

Lao Tzu – Chinese philosopher

Let me lay my cards on the table from the outset. The size of the business is far less relevant than the quality of the business. Ideally, you should seek both, and just in case your mind is wandering, we are talking strictly about investing here.

'Sex is one of the most wholesome, beautiful and natural experiences that money can buy.'

Steve Martin – American actor/comedian

GO SMALL, LARGE AND EVEN SUPER-SIZE THE DEAL

There are advantages and disadvantages to owning shares in a large company, or a small company. It is reasonable to regard a company like Coca Cola with its long history, capable management, powerful brand and truly vast financial resources to be a relatively safe large global company, whilst a small technology firm that is just starting off may be regarded as a much higher risk due to its lack of financial resources, short history, untested management and so on. So is it a good idea to buy just big companies? No.

The simple reason for this is that big companies were once small, and small companies may become big. So should you buy small companies only? No.

The simple reason for that is that many small companies will never become big companies because they are small and relatively vulnerable. So should you buy big companies because they are less vulnerable? No. Should you buy big and small companies? Yes and no. What you should be looking for are big companies with the capacity to become bigger, and small companies that can do the same.

Whilst it is true that a larger business may be more stable (depending on the business of course), there is a well known quote from Jim Slater mentioned earlier that 'elephants don't gallop', referring to the lower growth potential for larger companies. However, mice don't run marathons either. It is also true that when elephants fall over, they fall fast and have a big impact. Some of the world's largest companies have fallen and fallen fast.

Some examples include:
- Lehman Brothers Holdings Inc.: 15 September 2008: $691.06 billion
- Washington Mutual Inc.: 26 September 2008: $327.91 billion
- WorldCom Inc.: 21 July 2002: $103.91 billion
- General Motors Corp.: 1 June 2009: $91.05 billion
- Enron Corp.: 2 December 2001: $65.50 billion
- Conseco Inc.: 17 December 2002: $61.39 billion
- Pacific Gas and Electric Co.: 6 April 2001: $36.15 billion
- Texaco Inc.: 12 April 1987: $34.94 billion

QUALITY MATTERS MORE THAN SIZE

So if you think that size guarantees stability or reduces risk, you should remember that it only seems that way. What really matters is the quality of the company, and I keep going on about that because it is really what matters. Each of the companies listed above failed for different reasons at different times, but the point is this: if you had all of your money in shares in WorldCom Inc., your wealth would have been devastated. If you had all of your wealth in shares in the financial sector alone in 2008, the chances are that your wealth would also have been devastated.

We can learn something from the tale of master investor Aunt Mabel

The Tale Of Master Investor, Great Aunt Mabel

Over time, high quality companies will keep growing, keep increasing their dividends, and a relatively small investment will turn into a giant retirement nest-egg.

It all sounds good. We've all heard stories about how Great Aunt Mabel bought shares in GlaxoSmithKline (LSE: GSK) way back in the early days when they were nothing more than a tiny biotech, and how she held onto them all the way to her death at the ripe old age of 94, whereupon it was discovered she was a millionaire.

Cue wild celebrations amongst her kids, and profiles of 'Super Investor Great Aunt Mabel' in national newspapers.

The bottom line however is that Great Aunt Mabel was a reckless investor who simply became very lucky. She took a huge risk in buying shares in some loss-making biotech company. The chances of her losing all her money were much greater than they were of her becoming a millionaire.

Bruce Jackson, *Motley Fool*

HOW CAN WE APPLY WHAT THIS MEANS?

The solution is to manage your exposure to such risks by owning shares in both large and small companies, and making sure that you invest in quality companies only, from the best information that you have at your disposal. That way you will build the best defence you can against being over-exposed to a fluctuation in one market such as banking, whilst hopefully capitalising on a growing market elsewhere.

Equally important is taking a global perspective. It took around two weeks for swine flu to spread across the planet, a pace that even McDonalds would struggle to match, but the reality of our globally-connected world is very much something the investor must consider.

CHAPTER 17:

A global perspective

'The wide world is all about you; you can fence yourselves in, but you cannot forever fence it out.'

J. R. R. Tolkien – English writer

THERE IS NO MIDDLE EARTH

With investing you cannot think in terms of national borders. I have a preference for shares that have a global dimension about them. I feel somewhat vindicated in this approach when I see the scale of national debt that the UK is building up and read more and more about the state of the UK current and future finances. Just as it is not a great idea to have all of your shares in one large company, it is not a great idea to have all of your money linked to the success of one country and its economy, for they are subject to the changing economic tides in the same way that a business can be.

AS YOUR KNOWLEDGE AND EXPERIENCE GROWS, CONSIDER BUYING SHARES THROUGH FOREIGN STOCK EXCHANGES

It is very easy to buy shares through foreign exchanges.

I don't just buy shares traded through the London Stock Exchange (LSE); I also buy shares through the American National Association of Securities Dealers Automated Quotations (NASDAQ). Additionally, I have a preference for companies that operate in an international dimension and have exposure to global markets.

Several recent investments I have made include buying shares in asset management companies who invest in companies in specific Far Eastern regions such as Singapore and China. During 2008, a lot of the world's wealth headed east. If it does indeed turn out that for the next 50 years the economies of China and certain other Eastern nations will provide the most economic growth, then it makes sense that you should consider trying to own a part of that growth; but do so cautiously and consistently with your personal rules for investing. I have taken a small and cautious step in this direction.

Consistent with the arguments that I have tried to develop through this book, you should trust your instinct and never get drawn into following the hype. For the past couple of years the world of investing has been filled with commentators making case after case as to why everyone should invest in China and why that is where the smart money is, often citing the very high growth rates in recent years in the Chinese economy. Well maybe, but as always, there is another perspective.

CHINA MAY NOT BE THE FUTURE

Reflect on the following argument

Consider entering a sprint race with the world's fastest man. The world's fastest man is allowed to start ten seconds before you do. After around eight seconds, he is nearly at top speed, and what an impressive speed it is. Commentators talk about his superspeed status and how other competitors have been left behind.

Then you are allowed to start, and off you go. For the first six seconds you are accelerating, and what is more, you are accelerating at a faster rate than the world's fastest man, who has hit a cruising speed.

Suddenly, the commentators notice this and a frenzy of reporting begins. Some commentators claim that you have the potential to be the fastest man in history, others marvel at the speed of your acceleration during the first few seconds of your sprint, others produce reams of complex calculations with computers, and Harvard graduates show how, if you maintain this pace of acceleration, you will pass the world's fastest man in only a few moments, whilst others pour small fortunes into gambling that you will indeed become the world's fastest man. Then something else happens.

After eight seconds, your acceleration fades and your top speed turns out to be less than a third of the world's fastest man, who now starts to increase the distance between the two of you by a wide margin as each second passes.

Commentators bemoan your lack of success and those left nursing heavy financial losses on backing you as the winner wonder and wonder how everyone could have got it all so very wrong. Nobody saw that coming, right?

So why did I send some of my money east?

DIVERSIFICATION HAS MANY DIMENSIONS

I am spreading my bets and taking relatively small and calculated investments in businesses that will buy me exposure to Far Eastern markets. That does not mean that I think that everything worth considering is in the Far East; quite the contrary. I have far more confidence in the economy of the United States that started running well before the Chinese economy did. That said, I will continue to reflect and learn from patterns I see in developments on a global scale, and exercise judgement about where I should put my money. In doing so, should the economy of one country in which I own shares start to dangerously contract and offer only modest long-term growth potential, I am hopefully exposed to another where the growth is more satisfactory.

'Don't worry about the world coming to an end today. It is already tomorrow in Australia.'

Charles M. Schulz – American cartoonist

TRAVELLING GIVES YOU A NATURALLY-GLOBAL PERSPECTIVE. SO TRAVEL IF YOU CAN

Researching and travelling are two of the most successful allies to my investing career. Always take the opportunity to experience new countries and cultures as and when you can.

I had the privilege to be in China some years ago, just as they were officially becoming recognised as joining the WTO (World Trade Organisation) around 2001 and there was a tremendous sense of change and optimism about the opportunities that lay ahead. More than that, it was completely obvious to me that the Chinese were a nation of entrepreneurs, doers, traders. On every street I would see the way in which people were making a living for themselves. They didn't seem to have a culture or tradition of relying on anyone or anything else, although many of course work for businesses as elsewhere in the world, but the proportion seemed different to me.

I was also touched by their attitude to the world, wealth and success, which seemed very considered and healthy in comparison with many Western attitudes I have experienced over the years. The reason I even mention this is that experiencing China first hand gave me a very different perspective on things that has stayed with me to this day. I reflect and question my motivations and actions more when investing, and I retain a sense of humility about my success and I learn from experiences that disappoint.

> *'To travel is to discover that everyone is wrong about other countries.'*
>
> Aldous Huxley – English writer

I reflect on what I saw in China at that time and I drew my own conclusions about how it would play out and what opportunities I could see. I expected China to grow and grow fast and I continue to expect it to do so, but I also expect many Western companies and investors to face difficulties in buying into Chinese assets; and I think that China will have some way to go before its markets function in a healthy, competitive way. Coca Cola has recently had an experience that shows that, just because a country looks as if it is opening up and modernising, it may take a lot of time before it actually does so.

'China Says "Keep Out" to Coca-Cola.'

March 2009 – headline in *TIME*

So by all means diversify; it is a principle that will serve you well in times of adversity, but guard against getting swept up in hyperbole about China taking over the planet within 20 years. Nobody really knows how fast or to what extent the Chinese economy will grow. What I have noticed on my global travels is how people in each country perceive other countries, and just how totally wrong it can so often be.

This is where an informed global perspective can really help your investing approach to buying shares in many different-sized companies with access to many different countries.

PAY ATTENTION TO THE USA

Anyone who has travelled across America will know how big it is. Huge. Vast. I have shares in many American companies and I have a great deal of faith in the American economy which is why it was always my view that, as the recession that took hold in 2008 and started its global spread much like a virus, it would be America which emerged from the recession first.

My faith in the American economy is based on the quality of some of its companies, its wealth, its people and its natural resources. America is a staggering country, at the forefront of technology, vast, and with a truly huge amount of natural resources and talent. It is also a major consumer of the world's resources and very inefficient. The point is, having exposure to European, American and Far Eastern markets is a good idea. What proportion, and exactly in what, is where you exercise your judgement, having done your homework. Sometimes you will get it right, sometimes you won't; but when you don't, you will be less likely to suffer a financial disaster than if you had all of your eggs in a financial basket held in Iceland in 2008.

'It is better to be roughly right than precisely wrong.'

John Maynard Keynes – economist

CHAPTER 18:

Two apples don't make an orange

Just as we have noted some arguments to consider in investing in both quality large and small companies, and considering the opportunities both inside and outside our home country wherever that may be, we should also consider the value of investing in different sectors.

BUY INTO BUSINESSES IN MORE THAN ONE SECTOR

It is important to diversify your investments across more than one sector. Would you restrict yourself to buying from a range of cars from only one manufacturer? Or do you think you would get the best deal from being able to select from a range of manufacturers and their numerous offerings?

An apple gains no competitive advantage over another apple by being an apple, and it is just different from an orange. But put it together with an orange and some other fruits, and you have a fruit salad. What is more, if the apple was missing completely from the fruit salad due to an unforeseen and surprising apple shortage, your fruit salad could still satisfy. What is more, you may find out that it works better without the apple at all.

In case you are wondering what on earth I am getting at, I will clarify. You would be well advised to invest in more than one sector for exactly the same reasons as alluded to earlier; and by 'sector' I mean industry type, so retailing, banking, technology, utilities, construction, leisure, health and so on are all examples of different sectors. If you are not over-exposed to one of these sectors, you will not be over-exposed to any downside that comes from them whilst you will hopefully be positioned to exploit upside growth potential in another sector that is doing well. Mixing things up in this sense is a good idea. A fruit salad made from just apples and oranges is not great.

IT IS NOT ABOUT BEING RANDOM

There is no formula or set rule for this. It is really a case of what works for you, and what you are comfortable with, but always be mindful that diversification is not about randomly buying into companies in different sectors. It is about considered, intelligent diversified investments that will hopefully expose you to the best companies in a range of different sectors and of varying sizes. Equally, some will be broadly considered to be higher risk than others, and there is nothing wrong with that.

So by all means mix things up, but your core investing principles should be consistently applied. Great companies only, bought for a good price that is as close to a bargain as possible. Avoid at all costs following the herd, and especially when the herd is following a new sure-fire rapidly emerging opportunity with no past. Investment fads are really bad news and we will look into them next.

CHAPTER 19:

Investment fads – how they happen and why they are bad for your wealth

AVOID FADS

The world of business, be it management or investing, is littered with a history of management and investing fads – the vast majority of which proved to be just the latest in a long string of false prophets. Despite this, the world continues to fall for them time and time again. Why?

FADS APPEAL TO YOUR WEAKNESSES

Investing fads appeal to all of the characteristics that I have been so keen to point out as being bad for your wealth. Short-term views, quick gains, focus on vast wealth rather than realism that is grounded in the evidence, the latest, the newest, better than any other and you must have it. Fads belong in the world of the marketer, not the serious business person or investor. However, it doesn't matter how many people write about why they are nonsense, or how many people damage their wealth by behaving in that way, I know that people today, tomorrow and throughout the future will continue to be made suckers by such things.

There will always be a percentage of people who, despite all of the rational evidence and intelligent minds telling them that something is bad, do that thing anyway. We will now consider how we might avoid falling for the next fad and take advantage of the fact that most other people are likely to.

'Great things are not accomplished by those who yield to trends and fads and popular opinion.'

Jack Kerouac – American author

THINK LIKE A CONTRARIAN WHO HAS A TWIN THAT ISN'T

There is an old saying that if something looks too good to be true, then it probably is. From my experience, I think I could update that old saying by changing the word 'probably' to 'definitely'. You see, if you have done your homework, looked into everything you can, and something still looks too good to be true, you are probably missing something.

A fad will almost certainly be tempting and exciting and the real risk is when peer pressure kicks in. You see this in younger people especially, but many older people too. What often happens is that we abandon experience and knowledge of something that works and has worked fine in the past for the latest, the new, the next, and this is usually not at all proved and almost all of the time fails to deliver on its grand promise.

You may or may not recall the boom that took place in technology shares that happened as the internet took off in the late 1990s. Shares in companies that were internet-based grew beyond any reason. I avoided this completely, not by design but because I was only just getting started and was sticking to things I understood better, but most, even really experienced and knowledgeable, investors dived in. Only a couple of years later, they were drowning in losses they would largely never recover from.

WHAT WOULD YOU HAVE DONE?

How did that happen? Technology investments were the 'must have' thing, the latest thing and everyone else was buying them. Only a few people refused to go along with the masses and found themselves in investment-Siberia for around a year or two, but the world can change quickly, and change it did. In a short time, those who had found themselves in the sun found that cold arctic winds really wrecked their holiday.

After the technology bubble burst in 2000, the value of technology stocks had gone down on average by about 90%. That is one hell of a drop. Billions were gone. For some, those precious few who had the tenacity of character to stick to their inner beliefs and instinct and investing principles whatever the external cost to their reputation, well what a satisfying moment that must have been for them; and yes, the great Warren Buffet was indeed one of them.

'All human societies go through fads in which they temporarily either adopt practices of little use or else abandon practices of considerable use.'

Jared Diamond – American scientist

Buffet avoided this massive fad, and investing-suicide, by sticking to old and widely-known investing principles around what creates value and what doesn't. It should not be under-estimated how much pressure Buffet would have been under at that time to invest at least a few billion dollars in technology-related stocks, and if he could have found one worth investing in, he probably would have, but he couldn't and so in the face of huge criticism and pressure, he avoided the whole thing.

He must have been regarded as something of a dinosaur, a has-been, by the new breed of new wealth that had arrived so suddenly from this new world of the internet that promised a dawn of growth and which would create wealth the likes of which the world had never seen previously. For Warren Buffet, the alarm bells must have been deafening but to his dismay his audience was largely deaf, and he must have felt both isolated and saddened by the loss of respect he appeared to be suffering from at that time. How satisfying for long-term investors that his story shows that ultimately good guys can win.

HOW TO RECOGNISE THE WARNING SIGNS

Let's explore how to recognise some of the warning signs.

The world of management has been suffering an epidemic of fads for years, in my view, and for some organisations it can be a near-terminal experience. The trouble is that those brave enough to point out the potential short-comings of the latest fad, can find themselves very unpopular indeed, much as Warren Buffet must have been around 1999. Find yourself questioning a fad and you are likely to find yourself unpopular, criticised and made to feel intellectually redundant. Trust me, nothing could be further from the truth, so don't worry about it. Warren Buffet did the same, so you will be in good company.

A fad in investing, as in management, is usually identified by its tendency to promise quick change and reward. This key characteristic can then spread like a virus far and wide. If human viruses adapted to make us feel great for a few days before doing us in, they would be so much more effective. Some of these fads may become longer term, so they don't die away very quickly. Management fads arguably include things like Total Quality Management, Business Process Re-engineering, Six Sigma, balanced scorecards and so on. Some of them do have some value if taken in the right context by the right people with the right capabilities and applied in the right way, but in most cases they will fall spectacularly short of their promise. So what can we learn from this as investors?

Private investors buying shares are just as vulnerable to passing fashions as someone buying the latest fashion. Remember, today's trailblazers can easily become tomorrow's has-beens. Investors were piling into commercial property throughout 2007 and well into 2008 when not only were warning sirens going off in the minds of the more astute investor, but the signs were on fire as well. How many people should have known better?

INVESTING ISN'T SHORT TERM

You would be well advised to guard against any desire for short-term performance. That is speculation, not investing. The people who invested in technology stocks in the late 1990s and those investing in commercial property in 2006 were looking only at recent performance, which of course, appeared to be great. They were fooling themselves that it would continue and I am sure that in their minds a self-reinforcing set of beliefs and behaviours was starting to build up, not unlike an addiction.

Between March 1998 and 2000, technology funds broadly doubled in value and commercial property investments were making huge returns for a couple of years between 2004 and 2006. It is not difficult to see why these investments seemed so appealing to those who had already done well from them and those who still wanted to.

The belief that they would continue to do well was further reinforced by investment tips in the media, marketing teams and peer pressure etc. However, for me, a time span of anything less than three years is not even worth considering, and ideally I like to look into the history of a business over ten years or more. If you cannot easily access the performance history of a stock over a significant period of time, this should concern you.

IS SMOKING A DYING BUSINESS?

As we move through the opening years of the 21st century, social trends and fashions come and go as they have throughout history, and as an investor you cannot ignore them completely, because some of them matter. Take, for example, changing attitudes towards smoking. Smokers have always been a friend of the taxman and investors alike, for both have seen historically high yields from the tobacco industry. At the time of writing, the company British American Tobacco is paying a dividend yield of around 5%, but what was once an industry with a future is looking increasingly like one that now has a past.

I don't own any shares in tobacco companies and despite their apparent appeal and the great Warren Buffet previously being a fan of them, I will not be investing in them. Not for any moral or ethical reason as such, more of a business one; and speaking of ethics . . .

ETHICAL INVESTING, A FAD?

The opening years of the 21ˢᵗ century have also seen the emergence of a new type of investing, ethical investing, or putting money into companies that have a strong-values dimension to their business model. The Co-op Bank is an example of such a business and typical of a new generation of businesses which seem to be trying to tap a value-driven market. I don't intend to debate the merits of this approach here; my only concern with an investment is from a business perspective of what it is worth, what the return is likely to be and whether it meets all of my personal criteria for investing.

'I think animal testing is a terrible idea; they get all nervous and give the wrong answers.'

Peter Kay – comedian

BIO-DIESEL. I DON'T BUY IT

An example of what I currently see as a fad investment is bio-diesel. A couple of years back, I knew someone who had invested a large sum of money in a bio-diesel plant that I think was based in Scotland. Some initial arguments that were in its favour included the top management getting a loud endorsement from the Labour government for spending a lot of money investing in alternative energy; it had a new plant and looked as if it was set to exploit the new alternative energy market. There was only one problem: it wasn't making any money.

What is more, it had spent a lot of money. From memory, the last time I looked into it, its debt was around £100 million. It consequently went bust, and left the stock market nearly as quickly as it had arrived.

The time to invest in bio-diesel specialists is when and if they ever have a proven track record, over several years, of making real money and generating value for shareholders. As it stands, you would be speculating.

AVOID MARKETING SPIN AND ANYONE WHO IS TOO KEEN TO SELL YOU A PARTICULAR INVESTING APPROACH OR OPPORTUNITY

Beware of the latest 'big thing' or 'sure thing'. In the investment world anything claiming to be so is rarely the case. You should also consider why anyone would be keen to tell you, even if that was the case. There is a saying that in business three people can keep a secret, if two of them are dead. If any particular new investment opportunity was indeed a sure thing, that person would capitalise on it and become very rich, not dilute their profit by telling you and your friends all about it. You would be well advised to keep this point in mind when considering whose investment advice you take and how much weight you attach to it.

Also remember that, where fads are concerned, they tend to be in areas where there is inadequate robust information or intelligence, making them seem so much more plausible. In an industry of the future such as alternative energy, who knows what the performance of a company will be when its achievements are yet to happen? That is no different from the job applicant who states that most of his achievements are mainly in the future.

HIGH RISK DOESN'T MEAN HIGH REWARD. IT MEANS HIGH RISK

High risk doesn't mean high reward any more than danger means safe. Don't fall for a high-risk venture thinking that high risk equates to high reward. That can be total nonsense. High risk comes from not knowing exactly what you are doing, not someone telling you it is high risk and therefore the rewards are high as though the two go hand in hand. They most certainly don't. High rewards tend to go hand in hand with a high level of research, patience, tenacity and time.

The *Oxford English Dictionary* has defined a fad as something to which an exaggerated importance is attributed, and that sounds about right to me. Investing fads and management fads are one and the same thing in many ways; don't do business with either.

One aspect to investing that requires an equally cautious approach is the world of forecasting, and that is what we will explore next.

CHAPTER 20:

The future isn't what it used to be

*'If you can look into the seeds of time,
and say which grain will grow and which
will not, speak then unto me.'*

William Shakespeare – English playwright

BE CAUTIOUS WITH REGARD TO FORECASTS

I thought it worthwhile to write down a little about all of the forecasters and forecasts that frequent the world of the investor.

My online stockbroker provides a range of intelligence on any given company of my choice, one aspect of which is a 'consensus forecast' which is typically a summary of 'experts'' opinions of where the share, and the company, is heading for the next couple of years. Such forecasts can be based on quite sophisticated and complex methodologies. Shame they are largely useless.

The only time that I have found forecasts to be informative and helpful is when they appear to completely contradict my view of a potential investment. Their value in these circumstances is that they encourage me to look harder and further into the business, to see if I missed something. Aside from that, I am always reluctant to read too much into the forecasts of such experts.

*'Those who have knowledge, don't predict.
Those who predict, don't have knowledge.'*

Lao Tzu – 6th century Chinese philosopher

Economic tools have proved over time to be somewhat less than reliable from my observation, and I am not the only one who has noticed. Recently, Her Majesty the Queen asked some notable academics why the best economists at the London School of Economics didn't predict the economic meltdown that happened in 2008 and beyond.

Mr David Warsh wrote an open letter in reply to the question from Her Majesty the Queen which was published on several websites and in which Mr Warsh went to great length to point out that history is littered with figures whose advice, if taken, would have recognised the inherent risk and impending economic implosion that the world was heading into. He concluded his letter in the following way:

'Is it fair, then, to say that the present crisis was seen coming a dozen years ago by a man who died in 2003?

In any event, it is unlikely that we have seen the last of financial crises altogether. Kindleberger's book is precisely the horizon-scanning device desired by thoughtful persons, monarchs and commoners alike, so as not to be taken unaware and uncomprehending by the next financial crisis. Therefore, I have taken the liberty of asking amazon.co.uk to send the present edition of Manias, Panics, and Crashes to Balmoral Castle so that you, at least, need never ask your question again. In this, I am your humble and obedient servant.

David Warsh – Proprietor of www.economicprinciples.com

THE GREATEST INVESTMENT BOOK EVER WRITTEN

You can go back a long way to find wisdom that would have averted the latest financial shock to the world's economy. *The Intelligent Investor* by Benjamin Graham, first published in 1949, provides a framework for investing that, if followed consistently, would help the investor to avoid many of the pitfalls so prominent during times of market panic, and what is more, would alert the investor to signposts that the world is heading into dangerous territory in the first place.

'An economist is an expert who will know tomorrow why the things he predicted yesterday didn't happen today.'

Evan Esar – American humourist

Economic forecasting should be regarded with the cynicism that will be your ally throughout your investing career. It should not be dismissed, but rather should be viewed within the context of your intelligence-gathering and your view of where a business is heading.

'The only function of economic forecasting is to make astrology look respectable.'

John Kenneth Galbraith – economist

All forms of forecasting, no matter what science they are based on, are attempting to predict and model what is probable but not definite. Sometimes they can be wide of the mark. Consider the following predictions:

'Stocks have reached what looks like a permanently high plateau.'

Irving Fisher – Economics Professor at Yale University, 1929

'Very interesting, Whittle, my boy, but it will never work.'

Cambridge Aeronautics Professor, when shown Frank Whittle's plan for the jet engine, before 1930

'If excessive smoking actually plays a role in the production of lung cancer, it seems to be a minor one.'

W.C. Heuper – National Cancer Institute, 1954

'In all likelihood world inflation is over.'

International Monetary Fund CEO, 1959

'It doesn't matter what he does, he will never amount to anything.'

Albert Einstein's teacher addressing his father about Albert, 1895

LOOK FOR PATTERNS

No matter how eminently qualified a person appears to be, or the conviction of their beliefs, learn from the past and apply its logic to the present and likely future situation for yourself. If house prices increase in the future at a rate that places them above and beyond most people's capability to buy, based on average earnings and other measures, it could be time to get out of property-related shares and those who finance it. If it seems likely the world is heading into a recession, you may wish to check the levels of debt that companies you own shares in have in order to assess how exposed that business is to a possible reduction in available credit. If shares have been rising and rising for several years, you may wish to consider whether it is really the best time to be buying more, or is it the case that the market is over-heating and is shortly to start heading southwards at a rapid rate? If so, the shares you are buying today could be very over-priced in the near future.

'The market crash of 1987 caught most economists, scholars, and investment professionals by surprise. Nowhere in the classical, equilibrium-based view of the market, so long considered inviolate, was there anything that would predict or even describe the events of 1987. The failure of the existing theory left open the potential for competing theories.'

Robert Hagstrom, *Investing, the Last Liberal Art*

It is worth considering that a market crash like the one in 1987 could well happen again. The crash of 1987 was in many ways much more complex than what happened across the world in the recession of 2008 in that its causes are more complex. A significant factor in what happened then, as was the case in the latest economic mess, was attributable to human behaviour. Specifically, how humans behave collectively under stress.

Panic can cause a herd-like behaviour even in those who consider themselves investors as opposed to traders or speculators, and this resulted in the largest one-day percentage decline in stock market history. Herd mentality also contributed significantly to the current credit crunch, in that financial institutions which should have known better started to ignore their tried-and-tested rules due to pressure to compete with others who were doing the same. Combine that with huge rewards for bad behaviour and it becomes a dangerous cycle.

These are just some words of caution and whilst I have made light of some of the more entertaining mistakes people have made about predicting the future, sometimes of course, people also get it right.

USE THE INTERNET

The internet is the greatest information source the world has ever known, if you can intelligently interpret what is useful from what isn't.

The internet has made a very large amount of intelligence available to investors who are assessing a particular business. However, data is very different from intelligence.

'Statistics are no substitute for judgment.'

Henry Clay – 19th century American statesman

Data is data, statistics and numbers and so on. Intelligence is the meaningful interpretation of the data from which you can make reasoned judgements about the business and share price. It is the latter part of this process which is so important as it is through that process that you will decide what the company is likely to be worth in the future, or rather, if you think the share price is likely to increase or decrease over time.

'Believe nothing, no matter where you read it, or who said it, no matter if I have said it, unless it agrees with your own reason and your own common sense.'

The Buddha

OIL PRICES

A good example is to try and work out where you think oil prices are heading and what that might mean for the share price of oil companies such as Royal Dutch Shell 'A'. One view is that oil will ultimately head up in price based primarily on the view that as the world comes out of recession throughout 2010 (if indeed it does), then the demand for oil will significantly exceed supply. Hence the price will go up. Whether it will or not, well, that is a matter for you to research and form your own conclusion.

'If you believe you or anyone else has a system that can predict the future of the stock market, the joke is on you.'

Ralph Wanger – investor

This book should nudge you towards conducting further research and analysis. For me, that is the fun part: looking for the evidence, researching a company, learning all that I can and seeing how my view compares and contrasts with the so-called experts. Sometimes we do agree, sometimes we don't, but without exception I trust my own instinct every single time.

'A stockbroker urged me to buy a stock that would triple its value every year. I told him, "At my age, I don't even buy green bananas."'

Claude D. Pepper, 1900–1989 – US senator, politician and attorney

CHAPTER 21:

Cost averaging

YOU DON'T NEED MUCH MONEY TO GET STARTED

One of the things I mentioned at the start of this book was that it is a myth that you needed lots of money to invest in the stock market, and benefit financially from doing so. Well, there is a strategy called 'pound cost averaging' or if you are in the United States, 'dollar cost averaging', and it kind of supports this view.

I say 'kind of' because like almost everything with investing, there is always a different opinion, and I should point out that, whilst I am going to take a position in favour of this approach (or at least an adaptation of it), there are many people who would point out, quite correctly, that there is a lot of evidence to suggest that it doesn't do what it says it does.

However, let me make my case and you can make up your own mind.

THE ARGUMENT FOR POUND COST AVERAGING

If you think that you can time the market, that is, know when the absolute best time to buy a share is for the best price, you are quite wrong. Nobody can do that. Not even the great Warren Buffet, although I would like to bet that he can get closer to it than most. No; in fact, it can't be done. So we are in the business of dealing with volatility and uncertainty, and volatility can be either your enemy or your ally, depending on how well you know how to manage it.

Cost averaging is really about risk management. Yes, it is that 'risk' word again. Cost averaging is quite simple and it controls risk for you over time. So let's consider how this works.

HOW COST AVERAGING WORKS

Let's say that a share you are buying costs £1 today, and you have £3 to invest, and don't know whether to spend it all in one go or spend £1 a month over three months. If you take the £1-a-month approach, imagine the following scenario. At the end of month 1, you have an investment worth £1. During month 2, the share price drops to 50p, so you own three shares at the end of month 2 at a cost of £2. In month 3, the share price goes back up to £1, so you now own four shares worth £4.

What would have happened if you had invested all of your money in month 1? Your investment would be worth £3, as each share you bought cost £1, and you had £3 to invest. By splitting your lump sum of £3 over three months, however, you ended up much better off because you could exploit the downward movement in the share price when it dropped to 50p, giving you twice the number of shares for your £1 at that time. You profited by investing small amounts regularly instead of in one go.

Instead of ending up where you started, your investment grew to £4, and what is more, you did better than Mr Lump Sum who went all in at the start, thinking he was clever. Equally, this process can work the other way where the share price climbs. Whilst in that scenario you are actually buying fewer shares as the price climbs, by splitting your investment into smaller monthly bits you are actually reducing the odds of paying an inflated share price that will burn you when, and if, it comes back down. In effect, it provides you with reinforcement to your margin of safety.

To me, this approach is a compelling argument in favour of why you don't need a large amount of cash to get started in buying shares. You really don't. I started in exactly this way, and it worked for me, but I adapted the approach. I didn't simply systematically invest a set amount every month; I just consistently invested bite-sized amounts as and when I saw an appropriate opportunity.

Sometimes that would be twice a month, then maybe it would be three months later before I would see a suitable opportunity again. It is really a case of adapting such principles to see what works for you, but what I will say is that whatever you do, don't just wade into the stock market and invest a significant amount of money in one go. If you really do feel compelled to do that as you just inherit a huge wad of cash, then my advice would be to put it in the hands of a professional to invest for you, or at least to pay for some expert independent financial advice.

LITTLE AND OFTEN CAN PROTECT YOU FROM COSTLY MISTAKES

Pound cost averaging also affords you the flexibility of making relatively inexpensive mistakes as you are starting out. When I first started, I was certainly learning a lot as I went along, and I still am. It would have been a costly error for me to have invested all of my money in shares at that stage.

However, I stress once again that it is about adapting these principles to suit your own investing style. Nearly every guide to pound cost averaging that you are likely to read will talk about investing a set amount every month. I think that is about as foolish as investing all of your money in one go at the start! If there is nothing worth buying, why should you feel compelled to buy something just to adhere to a principle? It doesn't make sense, but there is something of value in it if you look a little deeper. It is about investing regularly, but not necessarily monthly, just enough to ride the ups and downs to your advantage, small sums in great companies when the opportunity arises. This is one of the best ways to accrue wealth over time.

KEEP YOUR FOCUS ON THE BUSINESS ITSELF, NOT A PROCESS FOR INVESTING

Your focus should not be on systems or strategies for investing, your focus should always remain on the business itself. However, if you apply an adapted version of the pound cost averaging approach investing as and when the opportunity arises to buy into great companies in different sectors, as and when the company appears to be a bargain buy, this is likely to be a sound approach.

Warren Buffet doesn't, as far as I know, set aside a billion a month and invest it no matter whether he can find a company that meets his criteria or not. No. He waits. Admittedly he waits longer than most could handle, but wait he does and then, when an opportunity comes along that fits, he wades in with his own adapted version of cost averaging, but on a grand scale. He invests patiently and aggressively.

'One of the funny things about the stock market is that every time one person buys, another sells, and both think they are astute.'

William Feather – American author

This quote makes me smile and it is quite true. However, it really can work for both parties. It all depends on what the buyer is paying, and what the seller paid originally. Both can do well depending on the answer to those questions. A share in a quality company will rise over time, but then may fall back slightly and a seller may then sell at both a bargain price and a nice profit. So it is true, both seller and buyer can indeed consider themselves astute in those circumstances.

Investing regularly in great companies at a good price will serve you well and, if you follow the principles discussed previously, you should both develop your margin of safety in your investing and increase your wealth over time.

CHAPTER 22:

Some worked examples

I thought it would be useful, having discussed some of the simple approaches to investing, to work through how you might start to look at some specific companies. However, the companies I use as examples in the following chapters 23–30 are purely as a means of illustrating the process, and not intended as any sort of recommendation or endorsement of the share itself. If I do own a stake in any of the examples used, I will clearly say so for reasons of objectivity, by no means as an endorsement of the business or the share. You should be aware that when I do state that I own shares in a given business, I may have paid substantially less for the share than the current market price and therefore a bargain yesterday could be expensive today.

The purpose of this part of the book is to try and provide an accessible insight into the kind of measures and intelligence I focus on when looking at a business. It is in no way comprehensive but rather represents a few initial signposts to further investigation. It therefore represents the investing equivalent to a stream of consciousness process. I can't stress enough how this is purely the start, the beginning, of a process that is taken much deeper. In looking at a business in the following way, we are merely seeing it at surface level, and only a fool would invest on the basis of looking at a couple of simple measures. As stated many times previously, a little hard work is required in reading some very dull material such as company reports and financial statements, and doing a little research about who is running the business etc. None of this is difficult in itself and doesn't require you to have any accounting qualifications. It does, however, require persistence and commitment to consistently investigating each potential investment opportunity to the level required to satisfy all of your questions, and here is a key point.

DO YOUR HOMEWORK

If you do this, and do it properly, not just pretend to yourself that having skimmed a page at the back of the accounts and having read about the sporting interests of the head of finance in the business that you know the business from the inside out, you will have given yourself an advantage.

'Nothing in the world can take the place of persistence. Talent will not; nothing is more common than unsuccessful men with talent. Genius will not; unrewarded genius is almost a proverb. Education will not; the world is full of educated derelicts. Persistence and determination are omnipotent.'

Calvin Coolidge – 30th President of the United States

The advantage comes from having greater stamina and persistence in looking into the company in more depth than the next guy is likely to, and in doing so, you can not only

'It's not that I'm so smart, it's just that I stay with problems longer.'

Albert Einstein – scientist

place your investments more wisely than the next person, but increase the odds of 'beating the market' significantly in the sense that you will be more likely to do better than most other investors. This is what I have consistently achieved over a number of years, so I know it can be done, and I also know that it does not require any special talent or intelligence. It requires patience, some hard work and commitment. You will be relying less on luck and more on informed judgement.

Remember that, when looking at a business, you will, more often than not, be relying on secondhand intelligence that is largely out of date (if looking at company accounts, annual reports etc.). Things may be very different from how they seem. If something looks like a great opportunity and seems like a great way to make money, you should be just as cautious as when looking at something that appears to be a disaster area. That may sound odd but when you consider that, hopefully, you would be less likely to invest in a disaster area since your emotional intelligence would make you naturally cautious, there is a heightened sense of danger that your own bias towards what may seem like a great deal could impair your judgement about the case of that seemingly great opportunity.

To illustrate the point, you might be looking into a business that makes a particular product, and it has shown consistent growth and pays a dividend and looks under-valued and so on, but what you might not know is that one of its largest clients, on whom it was over-reliant has just gone bust and its future is now far from certain. It would be some time before this problem would appear in the accounts and annual report. Meanwhile, the deal might still look sweet through second-hand intelligence.

Alice: 'If I had a world of my own, everything would be nonsense. Nothing would be what it is because everything would be what it isn't. And contrary-wise; what it is it wouldn't be, and what it wouldn't be, it would. You see?'

Lewis Carroll – *Alice in Wonderland*, 1951

There are always going to be things you can't know and don't know about a business, but if you follow a set approach consistently, you will at least be aware of as much as you reasonably can before parting with your money, which of course, you want to see a return on, otherwise why bother investing at all?

REMEMBER THE KNOWN UNKNOWNS

Remember the quote from Donald Rumsfeld? It is the unknowns you don't know you don't know that can have the most dramatic impact on the value of a business, and sometimes no amount of research will offset that. Just be aware of it, and remember it can work both ways. I recently observed a share in a mining exploration business increase dramatically in a very short time. Sadly I did not foresee this or I could have made a fortune. What made the share price behave that way was one of the unknowns. We will explore this particular example as one of the worked examples we will go through shortly.

All of the intelligence we will use in the following examples is easily available online via a range of sources, be it your online stockbroker or other share dealing website or resource. The website of the company itself is also a useful resource, as part of being a public limited company means that such businesses have to make publicly available a knowledge bank of information. Some of it is very dull, but it is very important that you look into this in as much detail as you can. Try to locate the investor relations section of the websites of these businesses and take it from there. You should see a range of information available, and you might be surprised at what you can find out.

BECOME YOUR OWN INVESTIGATOR. YOU MAY BE SURPRISED BY WHAT IS IN THE PUBLIC DOMAIN

Dig deep enough and you will find intelligence on what each of the executives in the business is paid, what bonuses they are paid, how many shares (if any) they own in the business and what the net worth of that is, who owns most of the shares in the business (an important one for me, I am always keen to know whose company I am in, so to speak) and a range of other quite interesting information. Such nuggets will be hidden under many pages of very dull and largely irrelevant information, so a little detective work is always required.

Once again though, despite all of the reports I have read over the years, I don't think having an accounting qualification or similar would really have made a crucial difference. You can learn very quickly and quite easily how to interpret the basics, and you may be surprised at how easily you start to see into a business through this type of intelligence. At first it may seem a little like staring at the Matrix, but after a while you will start to see some patterns and messages in the data and intelligence.

One important point is that in the following chapters I will be referring to measures and ratios that can and do change over time, and whilst the methodologies of how to look at a business will remain the same, the meaning of the measure will not. For example, a business with a strong dividend yield today is no guarantee that it will be in future, and you should be aware of the constantly-moving picture that impacts on these measures.

Also please note that the charts I have used in the following chapters provide a view of the broad movement, or trend, in the share price, and are nowhere near as detailed as the charts you can access online or from your share dealing service etc. They are provided to illustrate the arguments only.

The actual figures for measures like ROCE, dividend yield and, of course, the share price, amongst others, used in the worked examples, will change quickly over time. You should focus on the process, rather than the actual figures. It is the systematic process of how we explore starting to investigate a business that is important here, rather than why the dividend yield is different today, to the one quoted.

CHAPTER 23:

Tesco

Firstly, let's take a look at the retailer Tesco. I should declare immediately that I hold shares in this business; however, this and the following chapters of worked examples are not recommending investing in any of the companies discussed. The purpose of these chapters is to illustrate arguments for and against each business explored, and to take you through some of the measures that you should consider when looking at a potential investment opportunity. It is intended to steer you towards how you might start to look at a potential investment.

UNDERSTAND WHERE THE BUSINESS CAME FROM

Tesco was first floated on the stock exchange in 1947. In 1995, it took over its rival Sainsbury's position as the number one supermarket in the UK. In 2000, Tesco launched a service allowing its customers to order shopping online. Tesco is currently expanding its stores outside the UK into areas such as the USA, Ireland, Malaysia, Poland and Taiwan, amongst others. It has grown into a large and quite diversified business in many ways, offering everything from car insurance to mobile phones. Most recently it has signalled its intention to become a mainstream bank.

Let's start by looking at a nine-year trend analysis of the share price of Tesco (Figure 4).

In the last ten years the average share price for Tesco has been around the £3 mark, and most recently the trend has been for the share price to be moving upwards.

Of course, the past is no prediction of the future. So the first question to start to try and answer is if the share is really currently over-priced, or is it, in fact, quite a value share as the business is

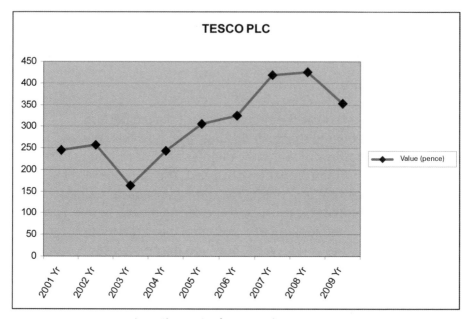

Fig. 4 Share price for Tesco plc 2001–2009

confidently marching forwards in a sound direction? It may look expensive in a historical average context, but if you knew that a year from now it would be heading towards the £5 mark or higher, it would suddenly look very cheap. Let's try to work out what might be going on with this business.

WHERE HAS THE SHARE PRICE BEEN?

In the last year, the highest share price that Tesco hit was around £4.15. Although there are many ways to assess risk and many different ways of scoring it, most brokers would agree that Tesco is a relatively low-risk share.

WHAT IS THE DIVIDEND YIELD?

The dividend yield on Tesco at its current above-average price is around the 3.1% mark, a better return than most savings accounts available at the time of writing. Tesco has an operating margin of around 5.9% (the proportion of the revenue that is left over after costs) and a return on the capital employed (ROCE) ratio of 12.7% (the higher, the better, and be very wary if you ever see a negative figure on this measure).

THE PE RATIO?

The price to earnings (PE) ratio for Tesco is around 12.5. This is a complex measure and much could be written about it, but my application of this measure is as follows. If this measure is less than around 10, it could be an indicator that a business is under-priced. However, it could also be because the company is in terminal decline in terms of sales or some other issue. Or it could indicate that a major asset has been sold in the accounting period measured or that a similar issue has boosted the earnings in that period. The point is, as with any of these measures, they cannot be viewed in isolation. In isolation, they can be quite meaningless or worse, grossly misleading.

However, in this case we know that Tesco has a PE ratio of 12.5. Broadly speaking, a reading of between 10 and 20 on this ratio can be considered to be fair value; and remember that the likes of Warren Buffet have always argued that it is better to pay a fair price for a great company, than a great price for a fair company. I totally agree with that view. So is Tesco looking like a great company?

IS IT GROWING CONSISTENTLY?

Since 2005, Tesco's revenue has grown year on year, as have its pre-tax profits. In 2005, revenue stood at £33,866 million and pre-tax profits were £1,894 million. By 2010, these figures had grown to a revenue of £56,910 million using the latest data and pre-tax profits of £3,176 million. Dividend yield has increased to over 3.5% in 2010. Whilst these figures will change over time as the share price changes and the business evolves, what matters to the investor is that you investigate and explore trends and messages in the data. Look for growth. All of these measures are heading in the right direction, so nothing of concern so far; rather quite the opposite, all quite reassuring. This is so far a consistent growth story but it is worth noting that the pace of growth has also been consistently slowing. If Tesco wishes to maintain its previous record, it will need to find a new way to grow, and it seems to think it has, but we will discuss that later.

INVESTIGATE THE PEOPLE RUNNING THE BUSINESS

Some people keep an eye on what the directors of a business do with the shares that they hold in the business. This can be indicative of something, or nothing. For example, a director suddenly selling what may appear to be a sizeable quantity of shares in the business might be indicative that he or she knows something you don't, and is selling before some bad news reduces the value of the business significantly. Or, of course, it could mean that he or she needs to take their spouse on a very expensive anniversary cruise and simply sold the shares to raise the funds. This is a matter of judgement. I only mention it as Timothy Mason, a director of Tesco, sold £22,230 worth of his Tesco shares at a price of £3.70 in August 2009. Historically, that is a high price and the cynical observer may regard this as a possible indication that the current price is over-heated and likely to come down in time.

The approach I take is one of caution, and whilst I try and buy the share at the best price I am likely to achieve, I really look at the business as a whole and ask myself if I am paying a fair price for a great business. You can't always buy something great for a bargain price.

DOES THE BUSINESS HAVE A LOT OF CASH?

One thing I always look at is the amount of cash a business has in the bank, and Tesco has lots of it. Quite a stash, but does it have any debts? The answer to this question is 'Yes', and quite a lot of them too.

AND DEBT?

Tesco has taken on a lot of debt, so that net gearing ratio may well be above my preferred threshold of 35%, but since I have already declared that I own shares in this business, I feel an explanation in this case is warranted. In short, I was prepared to offset my concern about the higher-than-ideal level of gearing in Tesco when I bought into it because I was buying the shares at around the historical average share price, and I believed that every indication was that the share price would rise, building a margin of safety into my investment, and I also believed that Tesco was growing, and growing fast.

This subsequently proved to be the case and, whilst they maintain more debt than I would normally be comfortable with, I do not regard Tesco as a normal supermarket. They are more than capable of servicing the debt in my view, and therefore I was willing in the case of Tesco, as with some of my other investments, to buy into the opportunity despite one or two measures not meeting my usual criteria.

WHAT THE BROKERS SAY.

You may or may not want to look at what the brokers have to say about a particular share. You should be wary, as discussed earlier, of reading too much into the opinions of others, but they can provide an interesting and motivating counter-point to your own and in that sense I do think they have some residual value. At the time of writing, more brokers were recommending buying Tesco than selling; quite a lot more, despite its historical high price.

As a side point it is worth noting how some external trends have surrounded businesses like Tesco. A strange phenomenon of the first years of the 21st century has been an odd reaction to large and successful companies, and Tesco has certainly been a target. When I am looking at investing in a particular company, I read lots about it. In fact, I read anything I can, and I spend a lot of time doing this. In the case of Tesco I looked into who was running it, what had been said about them, and I read anything I could that was written about them. This included books such as *Tescopoly* by Andrew Simms who painted a picture of a ruthless monopoly business destroying the diversity of community enterprises and limiting our choice, all of which was portrayed as very bad for all of us. Well, that was one view, but not one that I shared.

I saw a business that had reduced the costs of everyday essential items, and was ruthlessly competitive. Tesco was not always a monster. It got to be big by being better than its competitors. In theory, there is nothing stopping the man or woman in the corner shop from one day becoming the next rival to Tesco, assuming of course that they can find a way of not charging you four times as much for a pint of milk. Books like *Tescopoly* also portray supermarkets as soulless places where the elderly wander bemused and lost, like an extra from the latest George Romero zombie movie.

I feel this view is terribly patronising indeed to the elderly, a generation who in some cases have survived a world war, worked all of their lives and seen off a number of recessions and political and social shocks. To suggest that these people cannot navigate their way around a supermarket and that somehow it is preferable to have them ripped off by a corner shop, is nothing short of ridiculous. So, in short, I am a fan of Tesco because I am a fan of well-run businesses that offer value with limited exposure to risk. Tesco fits that description but that does not mean I would just buy it at any price. I have not bought shares in Tesco for quite some time, and I am currently watching it closely to see where it might be heading next.

WHO IS IN CHARGE?

So who is running this business and what kind of business is it?

From 1997 to 2010 Sir Terry Leahy has been the Chief Executive Officer of Tesco. His successor has been named as Philip Clarke. Sir Terry Leahy is a graduate in management sciences, he joined Tesco in 1979 as a marketing executive. He was responsible for the design and delivery of the Tesco loyalty card programme. He was appointed to the board of Tesco in 1992, and in 1995, it became the UK's largest retailer. He is rumoured to visit a Tesco store every week to see how it is being managed and is paid a salary of £1.3 million (using the latest information available).

From an outsider's perspective, the company is tightly managed, well run and aggressive. In Terry Leahy it has a highly capable leader who has appointed highly capable people around him – people who know the business from the bottom to the top and back again. That counts for a lot.

The following is an extract from the investor relations page of Tesco's website outlining their core strategy and approach.

Tesco has a well-established and consistent strategy for growth, which has allowed us to strengthen our core UK business and drive expansion into new markets.

The rationale for the strategy is to broaden the scope of the business to enable it to deliver strong sustainable long-term growth by following the customer into large expanding markets at home – such as financial services, non-food and telecoms – and new markets abroad, initially in Central Europe and Asia, and more recently in the United States.

The strategy to diversify the business was laid down in 1997 and has been the foundation of Tesco's success in recent years. The new businesses which have been created and developed over the last 12 years as part of this strategy now have scale, they are competitive and profitable – in fact we are now market leader in many of our markets outside the UK.

The Group has continued to make good progress with this strategy, which has five elements, reflecting our four established areas of focus, and also Tesco's long-term commitments on community and environment. Importantly, the momentum which it has given the business has allowed the Group to continue to grow well through the economic downturn.

The objectives of the strategy are:
- *To be a successful international retailer.*
- *To grow the core UK business.*

■ *To be as strong in non-food as in food.*
■ *To develop retailing services – such as Tesco. Personal Finance, Telecoms and Tesco.com.*
■ *To put community at the heart of what we do.*

What makes Tesco an interesting company for me is that apparently, its ambition knows no limits. Just as it was starting to hit capacity in terms of saturation of the UK grocery market, it started to look overseas. It appears to be a business that will not accept that normal business cycles apply to it. When Morrisons needed to grow, it took over Safeway which, in my view, was ill-conceived and a painful process by all accounts in terms of integrating the new business into the old one. Tesco has grown through careful and systematic strategic planning. By researching the company in great detail, it is possible to get a confident sense of where the company thinks it is going, and what is more, how it intends to get there.

WHERE IS THE BUSINESS HEADING?

So let's go back to my earlier point about where Tesco thinks it can go from here to maintain an impressive growth record. I have already mentioned its global ambitions, but the most interesting aspect of this business for me is its recently-announced intentions to become a mainstream bank. It has some obvious advantages in the banking business in that it is not currently a bank and is therefore bringing no baggage from the credit crunch with it. It also has a massive customer base, and a loyal one, by and large. Its bank branches could be located in-store, and could be staffed at flexible times to suit customers in a way that conventional banks seem unlikely or unwilling to do, at least until Tesco start to steal their customers. And there is the question, 'What would Tesco be worth if it was to become a successful bank as well?'

In short, there is no quick way of calculating this since it is entirely an unknown. The only evidence base on which to draw is the track record of the management team, and that is an impressive one. Tesco does not enter new ventures lightly and my view is that they will have done their homework, identified their core advantages and be working on an implementation strategy that will lure its customers away from their current main bank. The prize for Tesco is obvious. It would be the ultimate way of gaining the largest share of the customer's purse. Not only would its customers potentially have their salaries and savings paid into Tesco accounts, but by offering incentives, its customers would be more likely to spend more of their money with Tesco and all of its various offerings. If I was a mainstream high street bank, I would be watching Tesco very closely indeed.

So my view is that when Tesco ventures into banking properly, it is likely to be successful and that will in turn add value to the business, as will its expanding international dimension. However, my view is also that some of this potential is currently already priced into its share price at the time of writing. My investing style is to wait for a temporary storm to hit a business like Tesco, (much as it did when, at the start of the recession, cheaper stores that were perceived to be more downmarket such as Aldi and Lidl started to grow at a faster pace than Tesco and its share price suffered a bit) and then buy. As I have stressed throughout, I take the long-term view and therefore Tesco is a great business currently trading at a fair price. It is likely to increase in value over time and it pays a reasonable dividend. When buying Tesco shares, be mindful of its historical share price but also be conscious of its future potential.

'Only the Orkneys, the Shetland Islands, the Outer Hebrides and Harrogate do not have a Tesco store within their postcode.'

The Daily Telegraph, 23rd January 2007

Aside from that, it is worth noting that Tesco is sitting on a huge land bank in terms of assets. Also, Warren Buffet is a major shareholder, so if you did decide to buy into this business, you would be in very good company.

This big fish has left the little pond and is heading out to sea.

CHAPTER 24:

Amur Minerals Corporation

Firstly, I should make it clear that I do not currently, or intend in the future, to hold shares in the Amur Minerals Corporation.

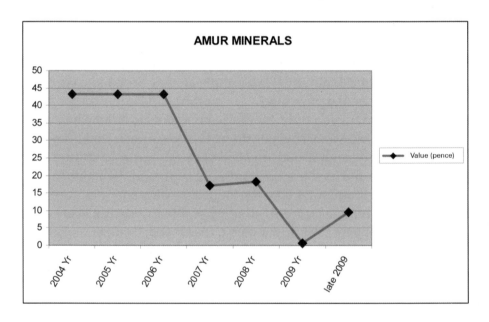

Fig. 5 Share price for Amur Minerals 2004–2009

Amur Minerals is in the mining sector and its latest share price at the time of writing is 9.25p (Figure 5). In the last year the share price of this business has been volatile, to say the least, in that it has ranged from 0.18p to 16.50p.

If you had been lucky enough to invest in Amur Minerals at 0.18p and see your investment rise to 16.50p you would have achieved a phenomenal return.

WHAT DOES THE BUSINESS DO?

Amur Minerals is an exploration company with its interests primarily in eastern Russia. The business recently submitted its reserve estimate for its Maly Krumkon deposit to the State Committee on Reserves (GKZ) for review and approval. A key aspect of this regarded the total contained copper and nickel which was valued at $1.8 billion and additional deposits which the company claims to be worth around $6.9 billion. Not surprisingly, this got the attention of a lot of speculators, and the share price rocketed by more than +370% in one day.

Despite that, the business is still valued at around £20 million. So there is something of an obvious gap between what the company appears to claim it is worth (billions!) and what the market appears to be currently valuing the business at. So is this a massive opportunity to grab a share at a bargain price that could go through the roof and possibly make you a fortune? Well, maybe; but probably not. Let's look at why.

LOOK AT THE DETAIL

The potential returns on the share price of this business could appear quite amazing and very exciting. There is no doubt someone, somewhere, made a huge return on Amur Minerals in this period, and well done to them. That said, someone, somewhere, won the lottery this week. You may also think that, in looking at a company with assets in the billions potentially, yet a value of around £20 million, you could not possibly lose. You would be dead wrong.

Let's look into this in more detail, rationally and consistently. This is a small mining company. Small mining companies are inherently risky and many never make a profit at all. What is more, this small mining company is working in Russia. Russia is a high-risk location, just ask BP. Politically and economically, to say nothing of the social instability of the country, Russia can potentially be a problem.

LOOK CLOSELY AT THE COMPANY REPORTS

For example, dig into the annual reports of Amur Minerals and in the latest one you will find reference to the political interference of the government in operating in Russia. If indeed Amur Minerals does turn out to be sitting on billions worth of resources, it is likely that they would be forced into working in partnership with a Russian company. Anticipating this, Amur has already started searching for what it regards as a suitable Russian partner. From an investor's perspective, none of this is good. Amur is keen to point out that it may not have to partner with a Russian firm, but it might, and the implications for potential investors could be significant.

WHO IS RUNNING IT?

Amur Minerals also has management and financial risk. Less than a year ago the management of this business proposed removing it from the stock exchange, and with it, your shares would have gone! However, if you believe that reward follows risk and you have an exceptionally high tolerance for high risk, you may wish to look into this business in more depth.

SOME KEY MEASURES

We have already noted the volatility in the company's share price and discussed some of the reasons why. The risk grade that most brokers put onto Amur Minerals is staggeringly high. If you consider that I generally look for a business with a risk rating of 400 or less, using the risk-metrics service of the HSBC stockbroker, and 400 would be considered my upper limit, the risk score assigned to Amur Minerals at the time of writing is 2,236 which I think is the highest that I have ever seen, even during the banking crisis of 2008. So it looks risky.

Looking at the return on the capital employed, the ROCE for Amur Minerals is –123.5%. You will recall that one of my principles is to avoid any business with a negative result on this measure. Well, –123.5% is negative in the extreme, although this should be viewed within the context of the mining and exploration sector where a negative ROCE ratio might be less unusual than in other sectors. However you look at it, though, for an investor, a negative on this is not a positive. Obvious really!

ANY DIVIDENDS?

Amur Minerals pays no dividend and this is unlikely to change. Many measures are not easily accessible when looking at this business, such as the price to earnings ratio, since it has never had any earnings. Yes that is right – it has never made any money. At all. None. There is no turnover to look at, and therefore any way of measuring the 'growth' of this business is pure speculation. That fact did not stop its share price soaring. Welcome to the irrational behaviour of the stock market and the importance of keeping your behaviour as an investor rational.

IS IT MAKING MONEY?

Since 2004, Amur Minerals has been losing money. Lots of it. For the year ending December 2008, it made a pre-tax loss of $2.3 million. Prior to that, a pre-tax loss of $1.99 million and prior to that $1.51 million, and so on. It does, however, have a flashy website where it describes itself in the following way:

Amur Minerals Corporation (AMC) is a rapidly-growing mineral resource exploration and development company focused on base metal projects located in the far east of Russia. The Company has three properties in the region with its principal asset being the Kun-Manie sulphide nickel, copper project located in Amur Oblast. With a JORC compliant resource of over a quarter of a million tons of contained nickel, Kun-Manie is one of the five largest new nickel sulphide discoveries since Voisey's Bay.'

At website: http://www.amurminerals.com/

According to its latest set of accounts, Amur Minerals paid nearly £900,000 in salaries, wages and directors' fees and some £234,000 in travel and subsistence expenses. Those sums were apparently spread over six directors. Six directors of a business that has never made a penny in profit.

I will let you form your own opinion of what that might say about the calibre of its management and its attitude to investors and their wealth creation.

Despite all of the reservations I have outlined here, which represent just the tip of the iceberg of reservations any investor should have with regard to this business, I am quite sure that in the days, weeks and months ahead many investors across the world will take a punt on this share. They will do so because of a psychological bias towards recent events, believing, quite wrongly, that they are likely to happen again purely because they just have. Believing that the share price of a business will rise again because it has just risen is no different from believing that you are about to have another car crash because you recently had one. That is not to say it won't happen, but the probability is no more likely.

Shares like Amur Minerals belong in the realm of speculators, or gambling, by another word. If that is you, fine. Not one for the consistent and intelligent investor.

CHAPTER 25:

Marks & Spencer Group

Firstly, I should make it clear that I do not currently, or intend in the future, to hold shares in the Marks & Spencer Group whom I shall refer to from this point as M&S.

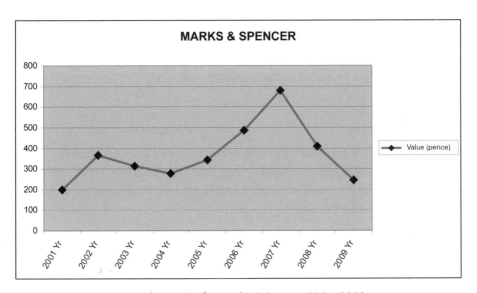

Fig. 6 Share price for Marks & Spencer 2001–2009

During the last nine years, the average share price for M&S was around £3.60 (Figure 6). Look at the price range for the share in the past year and beyond, and consider the current price within that context.

THE BUSINESS BACKGROUND

M&S is a high street retail chain that first took formation as a retail venture in 1894, and became a listed company in 1926. The company generates most of its business from UK clothing and retail sales. M&S has over 400 stores throughout the UK and a further 150 internationally.

Most stockbrokers view the share as relatively low risk, with my own stockbroker (HSBC) grading the risk of the business at 147, a score well below my personal risk threshold.

DOES IT PAY A DIVIDEND?

M&S has a dividend yield of around 5.3% currently, although this is forecast to drop in future. The return on the capital employed for M&S is a positive 17.3%. Its price to earnings ratio is currently 12 indicating that the current share price could be considered a fair price for this business. The question for me is whether it is a fair price for a great business, or a fair price for a fair business. Let's dig a little deeper.

THE PE RATIO

The forecast price to earnings ratio (PE ratio), as opposed to the current one, is 13.8, which could mean that the direction of travel for the share price is towards the more costly, or to put it another way, potentially less of a bargain.

BROKER RECOMMENDATIONS

A quick scan of broker recommendations for this share is a good indicator of why broker recommendations can be quite useless, with as many recommending it as a 'buy' as a 'strong sell'. You would think that one of them must be wrong, but which?

ADDITIONAL MEASURES TO CONSIDER

Let's look at the fundamentals. Revenue growth has stalled somewhat in the last three years following a period of growth prior to that, and operating profit is down significantly in the latest period measured. M&S has a reasonable amount of cash in the bank with over £422 million. That said, it also has a lot of debt with over £940 million in borrowings and net gearing in excess of my preferred benchmark of a 35% ceiling.

WHO IS RUNNING THE BUSINESS AND WHAT IS THE TRACK RECORD OF THE MANAGEMENT?

So what about its management? For me, this is where M&S starts to run into trouble from an investor's perspective. The company has had a troubled history in the last 20 years. When the company made the decision to switch from UK to overseas suppliers, it cost the company dearly and it has never really recovered from this. Additionally, its refusal to accept credit cards before 2000 was another move that showed the company to be burdened with a management culture based in the past, and less relevant for the future.

In the most recent years, M&S has struggled to gain new market share and reinvent itself. Philip Green attempted to take over M&S in 2004, and it has lumbered on like a listing galleon to date. The Chairman of Marks & Spencer is Sir Stuart Rose who was CEO until May 2010 when Marc Bolland was appointed to the Chief Executive role. It is too early to estimate the impact of Marc Bolland at this stage but shareholders will be hoping that he demonstrates added value to the business as it goes forward. A detailed CV for both can be accessed from the company website.

Since taking on the lead role at M&S, Stuart Rose has had something of a turbulent time and has delivered mixed results. 2008 saw the issue of a profits warning and the share price has been volatile. So where is the business going?

WHAT DOES THE FUTURE HOLD FOR M&S?

For me, that is the big question with M&S. If I wander into one of its stores and observe it, its clients look no different from those who were wandering around it when I was a kid, only now there appears to be a lot fewer of them. Despite a slickly-presented and professional advertising campaign clearly designed to appeal to a younger and sexier generation, step into an M&S store and it can feel as though you are stepping into a time machine set to 1986. The point I am making is that, for me at least, the business has not proved itself capable of change. Its management has failed to demonstrate how their leadership will add value to shareholders and I see no clear strategy that will deliver future sustainable growth. However, my views are controversial in that plenty of people keep buying its shares. I wonder when the last time was that these same people walked into an M&S store.

However, the business is regarded as relatively low risk by most brokers. I disagree with that and would give M&S a much higher risk rating than most brokers seem willing to. For me, there is a danger that M&S could become the Woolworths of clothing, with nobody able to answer why they would need to shop there specifically.

The customer profile seems to have remained largely the same, and therefore the investor considering M&S would be well advised to look very deep into the business indeed, before making an informed decision as to buy or not. As part of this process, I would recommend reading *The Rise and Fall of Marks & Spencer* by Judi Bevan, and really do look long and hard at their reports, accounts and plans.

CHAPTER 26:

AstraZeneca

As previously, I should point out that I do not currently own shares in AstraZeneca, although this business is on a list of companies which I place under special scrutiny and I continue to monitor it closely.

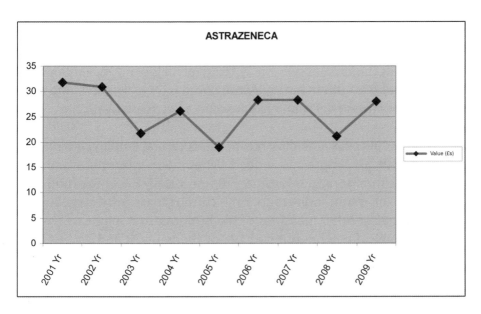

Fig. 7 Share price for AstraZeneca 2001–2009

The average share price for AstraZeneca in the last nine years was around the £25.50 mark (Figure 7). Check the current share price against the historical context of where it has been. Look at the range of fluctuation in the price and always consider the current price within that context.

A LITTLE BACKGROUND ABOUT THE BUSINESS

AstraZeneca is a world leading pharmaceutical group created in 1999 by the merger of Sweden's Astra and the UK's Zeneca which had been demerged from chemicals group ICI in 1993. Approximately half of its total sales come from the USA. Over a third of its revenues come from its gastrointestinal treatments such as Prilosec (Losec) and Nexium. The business employs over 65,000 people worldwide. Among its major shareholders is Barclays Bank.

RISKY?

Most brokers regard AstraZeneca as relatively low risk with a risk grade from HSBC at the time of writing of 103, well below my maximum tolerance band on this measure. AstraZeneca pays a dividend, and a good one at around 4.5% and it is forecast to increase over time.

This business also has a healthy return on its capital employed with a ROCE of 106.6%, impressive indeed. What is also interesting is that its price to earnings ratio is less than 10, specifically 8.9 at the time of writing. This might indicate that the current share price is cheap when set against other measures of the business, so it might be a value share. Certainly if you bought it at £28 or thereabouts and it went up to £35 in the near future, most investors would be thrilled.

ALL SECTORS ARE DIFFERENT. THE SAME RULES DO NOT APPLY TO ALL

A word of caution amongst all of these impressive results for AstraZeneca, and that is that businesses in this sector rely very heavily on their patents for drugs and treatments. These can and do expire. Anyone considering investing in a business should fully understand and research that sector to the best of their ability. You don't need to be a scientist. As I stated much earlier, you just need to be able to read the reports from the business itself. Most of the answers you will be looking for are to be found there, albeit hidden towards the back somewhere, in all probability.

BROKER RECOMMENDATIONS, HELPFUL AS EVER

Broker recommendations about this share are once again split but with more recommending it as 'a strong buy' than recommending it as 'a sell'. To the potential investor this is once again quite unhelpful and quite meaningless.

HOW IS THE BUSINESS DOING?

Looking at revenue figures for the last five years, impressive results are once again noted. Revenue has consistently grown and by large quantities, from $21,426 million in 2004 to $31,601 million by 2008. With the exception of 2007, pre-tax profit has also consistently grown from $4,844 million in 2004 to $8,681 million by 2008. The business has large cash reserves and net gearing of 38.94% which is not too far wide of the ceiling of 35% I normally adhere to.

2010 is already looking good for AstraZeneca with its share price boosted by successful defence of its patents in court, and continual growth reported in both its revenue streams and pre-tax profit.

WHO IS RUNNING IT AND WHAT ARE THEY LIKE?

AstraZeneca appears to have consistent and high-quality management with substantial experience and a proven track record of results.

FINAL THOUGHTS

AstraZeneca is a business that I have been watching for some time, and will continue to do so. I would already be a shareholder were it not for a lack of resources available to commit to it at the time that its shares were at barely over £20 in early 2009, but I missed the boat as I was committed to other investments. Whilst it is still a fair price for a great company in many ways, my view is that my margin of safety at over £28 a share is small and that increases the risk on the investment. I am therefore playing a very patient waiting game with this business and will buy into it when and if the time is right, and I may have to wait a long time.

CHAPTER 27:

William Hill

'There is a very easy way to return from a casino with a small fortune: go there with a large one.'

Jack Yelton

I should state from the start that I own shares in William Hill.

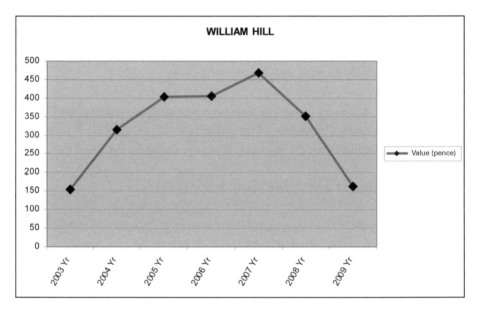

Fig. 8 Share prices for William Hill 2003–2009

SOME COMPANY BACKGROUND

William Hill is a UK bookmaker that was founded in 1934 and now has a chain of approximately 2,300 betting shops in total and around 25% of its target market. The business operates in all sports including football, greyhound racing, horse racing and so on, as well as a wider range of specialised betting. William Hill claims to be the biggest telephone betting group in the world. The company employs over 15,000 people in the UK, Ireland, Israel and Bulgaria.

WHERE HAS THE SHARE PRICE BEEN?

In the last seven years, the average share price for William Hill has been around the £3 mark (Figure 8). At the time of writing, the share price for William Hill is £1.85, well below the historical average. In the last year, the share price has ranged from £1.09 to £2.32, quite a dramatic range and great for anyone who bought in at the low point. In less than a year they would have more than doubled their money.

IS WILLIAM HILL WORTH A GAMBLE?

Most brokers regard William Hill as relatively low risk, with HSBC assigning the business with a risk grade of 196 at the time of writing, well within the limits of my tolerance level for this measure.

DOES IT PAY A DIVIDEND?

William Hill normally pays a dividend of around 3.2% and most brokers are forecasting a dividend yield in excess of 5% which is a good level, but the past year has seen a break in the dividend performance of this business as it conducted a rights issue to assist in the re-financing of its debts, and we will discuss that later.

SOME ADDITIONAL MEASURES TO CONSIDER

The return on the capital employed in the business shows a ROCE of 288.7%, so it should be quite profitable in theory! The price to earnings result for William Hill is currently reported at around 5.3, indicating that the business is possibly a value buy in that it may be under-priced.

'You know horses are smarter than people. You never heard of a horse going broke betting on people.'

Will Rogers – cowboy

IS IT GROWING?

'*You cannot beat a roulette table unless you steal money from it.*'

Albert Einstein – scientist

If we look at the revenue figures for William Hill going back to 2004, we can see that they have consistently grown year on year from £631.2 million in 2004 to £963.7 million in 2008. Pre-tax profit has been a little more volatile but the overall pattern has been an upward one from £207.4 million in 2004 to £293.3 million in 2008, and it is the overall pattern that you should focus on. The business has around £76 million in cash in the bank; however, borrowings show a downside to what is otherwise looking like a solid business. 2009 accounts show a drop in pre-tax profits against the historical trend, but within the overall context of this business it doesn't in itself raise alarm.

THE DEBT SITUATION

William Hill has a lot of debt. Not far short of £1 billion of it to be precise. This gives the company a current net gearing ratio of around 70%. This is well beyond my preferred threshold for levels of debt in an investment. Most recently the management team at William Hill have been attempting to reduce the level of debt in the business and in 2009 held a rights issue to raise funds to reduce its overall debt levels.

A rights issue is where a company offers existing shareholders the right to buy additional shares at a preferential price. Such events invariably result in the 'normal' market price for the share in the business to go down for a while, and as a shareholder facing a rights issue, you would need to consider your margin of safety carefully when evaluating whether a share price in a rights issue is actually a bargain or not.

The rights issue conducted by William Hill in 2009 was broadly deemed to be a success and will assist the business in reducing its levels of debt, something critical to its future success.

WHO'S IN CHARGE?

The Chief Executive of William Hill is Ralph Topping who was paid a basic salary of £477,500 in 2008. He was appointed to his current position of Chief Executive in 2008 and prior to that appears to have held many positions within the William Hill organisation. It is reasonable to assume that by the age of 57 he should know a thing or two about the business. Let's look at their strategy.

Strategy

William Hill's operations are based around three channels: online, retail (betting shops) and telephone betting.

Retail – The William Hill brand is well known on most high streets in the UK and Ireland. This is a mature market with high barriers to entry and we have established a market leading position by taking advantage of opportunities such as extended opening hours and gaming machines. This business has, by its nature, high fixed costs and we focus strongly on costs and capital efficiency to ensure the business continues to return good profits and cashflow. Where opportunities exist to broaden the retail offering in mainland Europe, we do and will pursue them.

Telephone – this business has seen some contraction as online betting has grown. Nonetheless there are opportunities to improve profit performance with a greater focus on cost and efficiency. Customer segmentation initiatives will also help to improve return on investment.

Online – this new and expanding market provides a significant growth opportunity. William Hill Online will take the business beyond its traditional UK borders, and will open us up to new, generally younger customers in new territories. It will also enable us to service our existing customer base better through improved marketing and customer relationship management, and to offer our sports betting service to a wider European audience.

DO YOUR HOMEWORK

Simple reading is all that is required, but you may need some expresso.

The following intelligence about the markets in which William Hill operates is taken from the various reports, accounts and information available from the company's website.

MARKET SIZE

In 2007, the UK gambling market was estimated at around £2.5 billion in gross win (the amount remaining once all customers' winning bets are paid). This is based on Government Betting Duty revenues of £373m at a rate of 15% (source: HMRC), and includes revenues from betting shops, telephone betting and those online businesses based in the UK.

THE COMPETITION AND WILLIAM HILL'S MARKET SHARE

Many customers tend to use more than one provider, so any estimates have to recognise that these same customers might also be going to competitors and indeed to different channels. Our estimates are as follows.

ONLINE

Online betting has a broad set of competitors, including William Hill, Ladbrokes, Totesport, Coral, Betfred, BlueSquare, 888, Stan James, Boylesports, Victor Chandler, Betfair and many more. According to global research company TNS in 2007, some 26% of regular online betters had a William Hill account, although many customers had accounts with other providers as well. Online customers are particularly likely to have multiple accounts, more so than the other channels.

RETAIL

In the UK market, there are five large players on the high street: William Hill, Ladbrokes, Tote, Coral and Betfred, who together account for over 80% of all betting shops. William Hill is the largest, owning some 25% of the total number of betting shops, and reaching, by our estimate, some 45% of regular customers.

TELEPHONE

For telephone betting, the same five companies appear, although there is also a significant presence from other, principally online brands, the main ones being PaddyPower, Bet365 and SkyBet. Based on TGI analysis (which measures consumer purchasing habits, media exposure and attitudes), we estimate that William Hill is the largest player in terms of usage in telephone betting, reaching some 45% of customers.

DON'T UNDER-ESTIMATE THE POWER OF A BRAND

So William Hill is a large player in the markets it competes in, and competitive markets they are. One of the factors that should not be under-estimated when looking at a business like William Hill is brand value. Just as a company like Harley Davidson has brand value, so does William Hill, although interestingly this does not always translate to brand loyalty as noted by the fact that customers who play online are likely to have several accounts for gambling with alternative competitors to William Hill.

ETHICS AND INVESTING: SOMETIMES THEY MEET

One additional issue to consider about this business is the very nature of gambling itself. Some people will take an ethical standpoint about investing, and that is fine. We live in a diverse world. From my point of view, investing is primarily about making money so I don't apply personal values to the process. However, political forces cannot be ignored and, equally, social trends cannot either. I see no evidence of societal attitudes towards gambling changing in a way that might be detrimental to a business like William Hill, something I continue to monitor.

BE AWARE OF THE ENVIRONMENT

Equally, political attitudes to gambling can change. The investor who looks a little deeper than headline messages about a business needs to be aware of the political and societal forces and influences that impact on a business. In the field of business strategy this would typically take the form of a simple PEST model which reminds leaders to be cognisant of the political, economic, social and technological trends taking place in the external environment, which may impact on a business.

CONSIDER THE FOLLOWING

For example, in considering a business such as William Hill and ten years of a government which has been favourable towards gambling, what might the attitude of a new government be? In an age of austerity, political attitudes to gambling may shift and you should be aware of that.

REFLECT ON WHAT ELSE YOU NEED TO KNOW

William Hill is a large and long-established business with a strong brand and it is profitable. It has a tradition of paying a good dividend and if it can put its current debt levels behind it as it is trying to do, and reduce them significantly, it remains a solid business, and one that I like. I like it because I know that people will always gamble. Whether it is the national lottery, speculating on the stock market (as opposed to investing which, as I have continually stressed, is something quite different) or doing 40mph in a 30mph zone, people will continue to gamble, convinced that they can beat the odds. In practice, they rarely do.

'In most betting shops you will see three windows marked "Bet Here," but only one window with the legend "Pay Out".'

Jeffrey Bernard – British journalist

CHAPTER 28:

British American Tobacco

First my declaration, I do not own shares in this company.

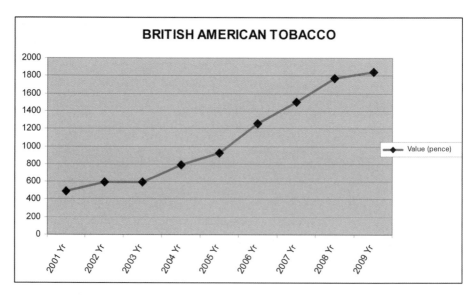

Fig. 9 Share price for British American Tobacco 2001–2009

COMPANY BACKGROUND

British American Tobacco was founded in 1902 as a joint venture between the UK's Imperial Tobacco Company and the American Tobacco Company. It is second only to Phillip Morris in the world cigarette market and has more than 300 brands sold in around 180 markets.

WHERE HAS THE SHARE PRICE BEEN?

As you will note from Figure 9, the share price has broadly been on an upward trajectory for some time. Between the year 2000 and 2009, the average share price for British American Tobacco has been around the £9.70 mark, although it should be noted that as the share price for this business has consistently grown over the time period measured, an averaged view of the share price is somewhat less valuable in this case. An averaged view of the share price is more relevant where the price has demonstrated volatility over a number of years. An averaged view of the share price of a company that has been consistently growing for some time tells you only what a good price may have been in the past, so is not that helpful.

The share price for British American Tobacco at the time of writing is £18.74 a share. In the past year, its share price has moved from £14.50 a share to £19.32 at various times.

WILL YOUR CASH GO UP IN SMOKE?

Most brokers view British American Tobacco as a relatively low-risk investment. HSBC's stockbroker service at the time of writing assigns a risk grade to the business of 95, which is very low indeed.

DOES IT PAY A DIVIDEND?

British American Tobacco pays a good dividend, some 4.5% on the latest figures and this is forecast to increase to around 5.1% in future. This company has long been a favourite for those investors looking for a steady income from their shares in the form of dividend payments.

ADDITIONAL MEASURES TO CONSIDER

The return on the capital employed ratio for British American Tobacco at the time of writing is 52%, a strong figure. The price to earnings ratio for the business is 14.4 indicating that the current share price could broadly be deemed to be a fair price for the business.

JUST OUT OF INTEREST, WHAT DO THE BROKERS SAY?

A quick scan of broker recommendations on British American Tobacco shows that most brokers currently rate the share as 'a buy'.

ARE MORE PEOPLE SMOKING?

Revenue at British American Tobacco has grown since 2004 from £10,768 million to £12,122 in 2008. Pre-tax profits, however, were £3,630 million and in 2008 they were £3,684 million. It seems this might be a business that is having to work ever harder to chase shrinking profit margins, or am I being overly cynical?

In 2010 we can see that the latest accounts for 2009 are showing a further increase in both pre-tax profit and revenue. This looks like a healthy business, no pun intended.

When you have to sell a lot more to maintain broadly the same income, you have to ask the question 'why?'. Like any investment proposition, you will have to look a lot harder and deeper than the surface measures that are readily available to you. But if you do, and there is nothing especially complex about it, then you will, in all probability, find the answers that you are looking for.

WHAT IS THE CASH POSITION?

British American Tobacco has a lot of cash in the bank, around £2,309 million, but it also has a lot of borrowings at £9,437 million with a net gearing figure for the business of 51.57%. This is above my preferred threshold for debt levels in a business, and when this is the case, I always look at historical trend patterns in the levels of debt serviced by the business. In the case of British American Tobacco, for the most recent three years of data available, the level of net gearing has been increasing. Whilst there may indeed be a business rationale for that, from an investor's point of view, increasing debt is rarely a good thing.

WHO'S IN CHARGE?

Let's consider the management.

What they say:

'We are pursuing a consistent strategy to build long term shareholder value for institutional and individual investors alike.'

The Chief Executive is Paul Adams who was appointed in 2004 before which he was a director. He joined British American Tobacco in July 1991 and held a number of senior appointments from that point.

Table 1 is an extract from the remuneration accounts as available from the website of British American Tobacco. It shows the payments made to the directors of the business and the Chief Executive Paul Adams who was paid a basic salary of £1,417,687 in 2008, but received total benefits to the value of £3,578,588.

WHERE IS THE BUSINESS GOING?

Always read as much as you can about a business that you are exploring and interested in. A key aspect must be their strategy. This is admittedly something I have a personal preference towards, as much of my background is in this area, but a business will succeed or fail based on the calibre of its leadership and their strategy.

The problem for this business in my view is its strategy. It wants to become leader of the global tobacco industry. That is its vision and in one sense there is nothing wrong with that. It is a big industry, at least, for now. The problem for me is that I can't shrug off the feeling that such an ambition is somewhat akin to striving to be made head chef on the Titanic. Whilst nobody can predict the future, it is hard to see how smoking is going to grow over ten and twenty years ahead,

Table 1. Directors' remuneration – audited

	Salary/fees £	Performance-related pay: annual cash bonus £	Performance-related pay: deferred share bonus £	Benefits in kind £	2008 Total £	2007 Total £
J P du Plessis	592,500	-	-	93,641	686,141	646,474
P N Adams	1,417,687	999,460	1,056,337	105,104	3,578,588	2,229,273
J B Stevens	528,901	356,992	372,329	96,565	1,354,787	-
N Durante	516,791	460,500	471,864	279,144	1,728,299	-
K M A de Segundo	88,333	-	-	16,651	104,984	18,796
R E Lerwill	98,333	-	-	19,102	117,435	95,515
A M Llopis	75,000	-	-	-	75,000	75,000
C J M Morin-Postel	75,000	-	-	-	75,000	18,750
A Ruys	88,333	-	-	19,763	108,096	75,562
Sir Nicholas Scheele	91,667	-	-	20,443	112,110	75,887
M H Visser	75,000	-	-	11,018	86,018	81,879
Former Directors						
P E Beyers	-	-	-	-	-	37,500
K H Clarke	55,000	-	-	46,450	101,450	173,909
A Monteiro de Castro	173,166	-	-	135,875	309,041	1,878,877
P A Rayner	644,683	626,792	20,798	241,476	1,533,749	1,444,257
R L Pennant-Rea	-	-	-	-	-	25,000
Total remuneration	4,520,394	2,443,744	1,921,328	1,085,232	9,970,698	6,876,679

at least in the West. It could be that as massive populations in rapidly-developing places such as China move upwards in terms of wealth and prosperity, they start to smoke in greater numbers, but somehow that seems unlikely to me, which is a personal judgement.

THE OVERALL VIEW

As it stands, British American Tobacco is a massive company, with large debts but an equally large turnover. It has grown its revenue but its pre-tax profits have not grown in line with that. It pays a solid and good dividend and has been a good share historically for those investors looking for an income from their shares.

Smoking is something that may have had its best days in terms of business. The future of this business is therefore likely to be dependent on its capacity to market itself to new countries and new markets, and its ability to do that will depend on government attitudes towards a product that can kill you.

CHAPTER 29:

QinetiQ Group

I should declare that I hold shares in QinetiQ group.

SOME BACKGROUND

QinetiQ Group is one of the world's leading defence technology companies. It manufactures and supplies a range of products including weapons, advanced robotic systems, port security products and advanced security for computer systems.

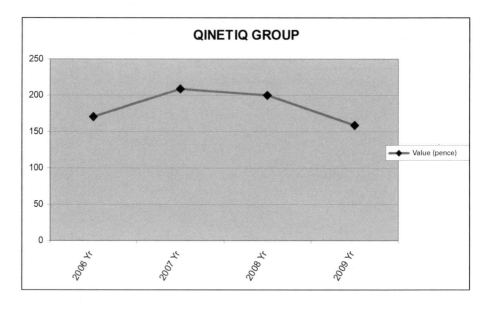

Fig. 10 Share price for QinetiQ Group 2006–2009

The above chart (Figure 10) hides the fact that the share price of QinetiQ Group has been quite volatile in the overall period measured since it takes measurements at four key points, rather than many measurements at various points during a particular year, which would show a more detailed picture. You can access a more detailed view online that will show a pattern that looks a bit more like cardiac arrest, but the general trend is as shown in the chart.

WHERE HAS THE SHARE PRICE BEEN?

The average share price in the period measured from 2006 onwards for QinetiQ Group has been broadly around the £1.80 mark. At the time of writing, the share price for QinetiQ Group is £1.39 below its historical average price. In the past year, the share price has ranged from £1.25 to £2.28, quite a large range of variation as alluded to previously.

Buying below the historical average price with a business like this is advisable since it will provide a margin of safety in what might be very volatile times. You should remember that there is no such thing as a 'paper loss'. A loss is a loss. The objective of buying shares is to make money, whether by accruing value in the form of shares or by selling them at a profit.

'There are three reasons to be in business. To make money, to have fun – and to make money.'

Theo Paphitis – entrepreneur

ARE WEAPONS RISKY?

QinetiQ Group is regarded by most brokers as relatively low risk currently, although this may change.

DOES IT PAY A DIVIDEND?

The dividend yield for the business is an acceptable 3.4% and most brokers are forecasting this to increase slightly over time. The business has a good dividend cover of 3.3% (this is a measure of earnings against how much the business pays to shareholders in dividends; it can be useful in assessing what margin of safety there is to the dividend should the business hit turbulence) and a healthy operating margin.

TAKE THE TIME TO LOOK AT AS MANY MEASURES AS YOU CAN

You can look into what measures there are and you may wish to look at many others besides the ones I mention in this book. The operating margin is simply the amount of income divided by net sales, and it is useful because it shows you what level of income is left before deductions. There obviously needs to be some in order for the business to meet its mandatory obligations in the longer term towards fixed costs etc.

The return on the capital employed (ROCE) for QinetiQ Group is 21.9% and its price to earnings ratio is currently 8.8, indicating that the share price might represent a value buy. Most brokers at the time of writing are in favour of this stock being a 'buy' as opposed to a 'sell', and that is most likely because it is currently trading at well below its normal historical price levels.

IS IT GROWING?

Revenue for QinetiQ Group has grown consistently from £855.9 million in 2005 to £1,617 million by 2009. Pre-tax profits show a similar trend and have grown from £78 million in 2005 to £114 million by 2009, although there was one significant blip in 2008 when it dropped to £51 million.

DEBT AND CASH

The business has £262 million in cash in the bank and borrowings that create a net gearing figure of 38.99% for the business, around the ceiling of my normal tolerance level for debt.

HARD AND SOFT INTELLIGENCE

As you have hopefully started to realise from these worked examples, you need to look at both the quantifiable data and intelligence at your disposal when assessing a business, and also the softer qualitative information. I am as interested in the strategy and management of a particular business, as I am in its financial reports and data. Neglecting one or the other can lead to disaster. They are two sides of the same coin so let's look at some of the softer intelligence.

ALWAYS LOOK AS DEEPLY INTO A BUSINESS AS YOU CAN

The following information provides some detail on the company background and is taken from their website.

In 1991, the UK national Defence Research Agency (DRA) was formed through the union of a number of government research organisations which, in 1995, became the Defence Evaluation and Research Agency (DERA). In July 2001, QinetiQ was founded from the partition of DERA into two separate organisations and, in February 2003, became a public private partnership with US-based Carlyle Group being the equity investor. QinetiQ was then floated on the London stock market in February 2006.

A presence in North America was established in 2001 through QinetiQ Inc. In 2004, the QinetiQ North America (QNA) division was created with its own board and management. Since its establishment, QNA has grown through an acquisition strategy, including the acquisition of Analex Corporation, Apogen Technologies Inc, Foster-Miller Inc, ITS Corporation, OSEC, Planning Systems Inc and Westar.

Europe, Middle East and Australasia (EMEA) was created as a division in April 2008. QinetiQ also has a separate ventures division to oversee the management of spin-out technologies.

By January 2008, three defence consulting companies had also been acquired in Australia. These acquisitions represent our first investment in Australia and are in line with our EMEA strategy to expand our geographical footprint into markets outside the UK and US.

In 2009 the Group continued its acquisition into North America through the acquisition of niche specialist capability areas. During this year the MOD sold its shareholding in the Group.

As can be noted from a little background research, QinetiQ Group has exposure to international markets and, whilst it is in the defence technology business, within that context it is well diversified. It is not just making bullets, for example.

WHERE DOES IT THINK IT IS GOING?

Let's look a little at the vision and strategy of this business.

Our vision
To be recognised internationally as a leading provider of technology-based services and solutions to customers in defence, security and related markets.

How we will achieve it
Ensure we have outstanding people, facilities and technologies available to provide innovative, high-value solutions to our customers' important problems.

Provide research, technical advice, technology solutions and services to customers in our core markets of defence and security, and transfer know-how and capability into important adjacent markets.

Our strategy
Build and maintain existing relationships.

Build on our powerful defence franchises through increased customer focus, growing our market share in technology insertion, advice and managed services whilst also expanding our presence into related markets where we already have a good footprint such as security and intelligence.

Develop selected global capabilities
Develop global capabilities in selected fields of service and technology.

Provide integrated solutions and service offerings across geographies.

Increase synergies across our business.

Strengthen and develop our international reach and presence

Continue building our business in our home markets of UK, North America and Australia delivering good organic growth supplemented by targeted acquisitions.

Build valuable new market positions in selected additional international markets including the Middle East and the Far East.

Maintain a leading position in key areas of defence and continue expansion into other adjacent markets.

Expand relevant international routes to market for defence technology applications.

Further develop security market potential, our energy and environmental offerings and applications to other relevant markets through direct exploitation, venturing and licensing.

Develop enhance and maintain our people skills and resources

Recruit and retain people with outstanding intellectual capacity, technical skills and personal qualities.

Motivate and recognise innovation in technology and problem solving and excellence in customer service and delivery.

Recognise and promote talent.

Further embed a customer-focused culture throughout our businesses.

I do have a bias towards a business that doesn't just state what its vision is, after all anyone can do that quite easily, but rather goes a little further in explaining how it will achieve this vision. The vision of a business is in essence its mission over time. It should be clear how a vision will be achieved and there should be some indication as to the expected timeframe.

THE PEOPLE RUNNING THIS BUSINESS AND IN PARTICULAR THE CHIEF EXECUTIVE

QinetiQ Group is currently run by Leo Quinn, the Chief Executive Officer. He was appointed Chief Executive in November 2009 and is a Member of the Compliance Committee, Nominations Committee and Security Committee.

Leo was Chief Executive Officer of De La Rue plc between 2005 and 2009. Before that he was Chief Operating Officer of Invensys plc's Production Management Division. Prior to that time, he spent 16 years with Honeywell Inc. in a variety of senior management roles in the USA, Europe, the Middle East and Africa. Leo Quinn was formerly a Non-executive Director of Tomkins plc.

THINGS ARE NEVER QUITE AS THEY SEEM

So is QinetiQ Group a value buy as it stands today? As ever, the picture is more complicated than the simplistic measures we have referred to here. If you were seriously considering taking a punt on this business, you would need to read the financial statements closely and read as much as you can about the sector that QinetiQ Group operates in. As we head into a period in history that is likely to be characterised by governments looking to reduce their spending after years of over spending, it is likely that in many cases spending on defence will be cut, not increased.

So where does that leave QinetiQ and might it be vulnerable? Well, the short answer is 'Yes and no', but more the latter than the former. The reason that I take this view is purely a matter of my own judgement but I believe that this business is well diversified. It is not just making fighter planes or tanks or similar, it is also involved in IT security and intelligent defence systems, and all manner of other security solutions. My view is that we are entering a period of time where traditional physical weaponry like tanks and bombs may be less relevant to future security than chips of silicon on a board.

QUALITY MANAGEMENT

The business appears to be a robust one and what gives me a degree of confidence in it is its current management. They have a proved track record of winning large contracts, and they are well connected. Many Ministry of Defence contracts land with QinetiQ Group. From my perspective, the shares are currently cheap, and the main reason for that is that many brokers are seeing it as heading into leaner times as the implications of reining in years of excessive government spending start to impact. In other words, most brokers are expecting defence companies to have to chase fewer contracts worth less money.

Governments can and will cut defence spending in all probability, but they will probably cut it less, proportionately speaking, than other targets and there will be winners and losers in the defence sector from this process. My view is that QinetiQ, at least for the foreseeable future, is a winner and I would not be surprised to see the share price exceed the £2 mark within the medium-term future. Not a bad return on the current £1.39 if it happened that way.

CHAPTER 30:

Interior Services Group

I do not currently hold shares in Interior Services Group, but the company is on a list of businesses that I keep under special interest and monitor closely.

Interior Services Group is in the support services sector.

WHAT DO THEY DO?

In their own words:

Interior Services Group delivers award winning New build, Refurbishment and Fit out services internationally with operations in the UK, Europe and Asia. The company's headquarters are in the UK.

As one of the most established and respected companies in the construction industry, ISG has been managing the construction process and simplifying the complex for owners, occupiers and developers since 1989. With a wealth of experience working across a variety of sectors, locations and project values up to £100 million, we offer a tailored service to every individual client's needs.

WHERE HAS THE SHARE PRICE BEEN?

Between 2000 and 2009, the average share price for Interior Services Group was around the £2.20 mark. Check the current share price against the context of where it has been. In the last year the share price for Interior Services Group has ranged from £0.85 to £2.06, quite a variation. If you had bought £1,000 worth at 85p you would now be sitting on £2,010 in less than 12 months, over 100% up. Easily said

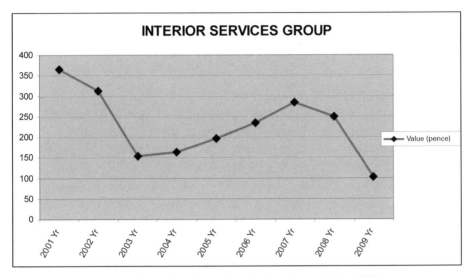

Fig. 11 Share price for Interior Services Group 2001–2009

in retrospect, harder to do in practice. So let's explore this business in more detail and see how it stands up.

IS IT RISKY?

Most brokers regard Interior Services Group as relatively low risk with HSBC currently giving it a risk grade of 179, well below my 350 preferred ceiling.

DOES IT PAY A DIVIDEND?

Interior Services Group pays a very good dividend, some 7.8% on the latest figures with a dividend cover of 2.7 which is acceptable. So in other words, 7.8% interest or income on your money. Most ISAs at the time of writing are paying between 0.5% and 3% interest depending on the respective terms and conditions. I am not comparing the two investments as like for like examples as they are not.

Some people may get pleasure from reading a book whilst others may opt for jumping out of a plane – some things are better suited to some people, but if you can manage to read whilst sky-diving, your money could pay you a lot more than where most people put theirs, if you are prepared to do your research properly.

A sum of £1,000 invested in Interior Services Group would pay you £78 in dividends at the current rate. The same amount of money in a basic ISA may currently pay around £5 a year. Quite a difference.

In case you are thinking you have never heard of Interior Services Group so it must be risky, you have probably heard of the oil giant Royal Dutch Shell, a company who has more money than most countries, and they are paying a broadly comparable dividend too. I will discuss how the concept of low risk and high return appeals to me towards the end of this book, but for now it is worth noting that, contrary to the common saying 'high risk, high reward', I will show how low risk and high reward are not mutually exclusive approaches.

ADDITIONAL MEASURES

The business is reporting a negative return on the capital employed with a figure of –60% on this measure using the latest data. There may be a number of reasons for this. Reading the financial statements, the business entered into a number of financial agreements such as taking on loans to expand the business in various ways and this cash may have been income-neutral until deployed for the purposes for which it was intended. Nevertheless, it would require further investigation, but for now it is something to note and not forget about.

The price to earnings ratio for Interior Services Group is 4.7 which can be indicative of a share price that is a potential bargain if everything else checks out to your satisfaction. Broker recommendations are unanimous at the time of writing in regarding this share as a 'buy'. As stated before, broker recommendations are background noise and if they seem to confirm what you are thinking, you are probably wrong and should look much further and deeper. Not that I have anything personal against brokers and their tips, it is more that I am guarded against seeking positive reinforcement for a behaviour.

IS IT GROWING?

Since 2004, revenue for Interior Services Group has grown more or less consistently from £361.36 million in 2004 to £1,090.08 million by 2008 with only one year, 2005, when it did not increase. Pre-tax profit however has increased every year since 2004 from £2.3 million to £12.62 million by 2008. Indications for 2010 are that pre-tax profit has slipped slightly but that is within the context of the recession and exceptional economic circumstances.

The business has £60 million in cash in the bank and has negligible borrowings, so its net gearing is zero in real terms. That is a lot of money in a business that has no debt.

What about the management?

WHO'S IN CHARGE?

The Chief Executive is David Lawther and this is what their website has to say about him.

David qualified at Durham University in Engineering Science and Management qualifying as a chartered accountant whilst working at Kidsons Chartered Accountants in London. Following six years at John Mowlem & Co PLC working his way to Group Treasurer, David joined the executive team at Wilson Connolly Holdings as Group Finance Director and was instrumental in refocusing the strategic direction of the group, realigning their products and expanding the group.

David is a non executive director of our partner in France and a Director of our corporations in Asia, ISG Asia.

In 2008, the total package paid to David Lawther was £646,322. The business has a management team with impressive CVs and are well connected.

Interior Services Group is a solid, diversified business that pays a good dividend and offers the potential for gains based on its current share price which is below its historical average.

CHAPTER 31:

Screening for value shares – low risk and high reward

'In God we trust, all others bring data.'

Dr W. Edwards Deming, 1900–1993 – American statistician

ONCE YOU KNOW A LITTLE ABOUT WHAT TO LOOK FOR, HOW DO YOU START TO FIND SHARES?

Set up an investment account

When you set up an online share dealing service/account, which I strongly suggest you do since it is the only practical way to select and buy your own shares, you will gain access to a range of tools and facilities to help you. You should not be daunted by the range and apparent complexity of them, as in most cases they are really quite straightforward and you will need to use only a few of the features presented to you, as most of them are largely gimmicks and of little practical value.

I have tended to avoid heat maps and graphs and anything that looks like a magic-eye picture and I focus on what I need to know, and for that I just need to use a screener tool. I have already decided the types of companies I want to invest in so I just need to find them, which is the fun part.

Make sure you have your own set of principles that will govern your approach to investing

Having your own set of principles should manage risk to an acceptable level for you.

A little secret: the well known phrase 'high risk equals high reward' is wrong. Yes, quite wrong. In fact, from my experience, low risk equals high reward and high risk equals high risk which usually means losing your money. Risk comes from not really being competent at what you are doing, such as by buying a share in a company that has never made any money, is run by a Chief Executive who pays himself a million pounds a year whilst the company has gearing of 80% and makes components for cassette players.

However, I do accept that risk is a matter of perspective and you should know yourself well enough to know what approach suits you. Statistically, flying on a plane is one of the safest forms of travel, but if the engines fail having just taken off, statistically, the odds are not great. Driving a car by comparison is statistically far more dangerous than flying in a plane, but if the engine fails whilst pulling off your drive in the morning, the chances are you will just be late for that meeting. It won't kill you. Unless of course the car rolls into the road and you are killed by an articulated lorry in which case you were probably not the sort of person who should be dabbling with shares anyway.

That said, I know people who are genuinely afraid of flying yet drive a car every day, and have even had the occasional accident in their car during their driving career. This is what I mean by a matter of perspective. If you want your finances to fly, you have to be willing to get into the plane and, assuming you have already put yourself into the 'learning to fly' category of people, it is all about not taking risks from that stage. Pilots in commercial airliners don't generally mess around but rather adhere to a consistent set of rules and processes, even when something appears to be going wrong. It is that adherence to a consistent set of rules that saves lives when something doesn't go according to plan, and it is the same principle with your investments. Consistently adhering to a set of principles that suit you will help you to select businesses that meet your criteria, and reduce the risk of you not achieving your objectives.

Define your own basket of measures, and stick to it

I use an online stock screener facility to target businesses based on a range of value measures that matter to me. This is not to say that the measures I look at are the right ones, or even advisable for anyone else, but rather they serve to illustrate the application of just one of the many helpful facilities available to you via online share-dealing facilities. Figure 12, for example, shows changes to the share prices of some key players in the banking sector over a five-year period and is but one example of the many types of intelligence you will be able to access in seconds and easily from most online share-dealing services.

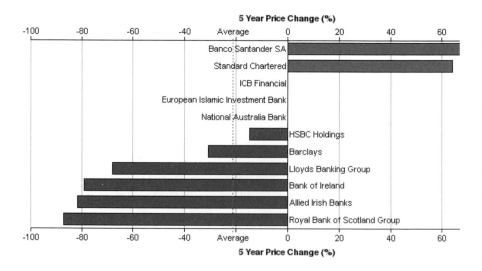

Fig. 12 Changes to share prices of key players in banking sector

Using a stock screener you can set it up very quickly and easily to screen out stocks for you that meet certain specific criteria. For example, you may wish to select stocks that have a minimum dividend yield of say 4%, a return on the capital employed ratio of at least 10%, a price to earnings ratio of less than 10, a dividend cover of at least 2, net gearing no higher than 35%, a risk grade of no higher than 350, and so on. You may also wish to set criteria regarding growth and select only businesses that have been growing by a specific amount for a given number of years.

The point is that having entered a few simple numbers into the stock screener, it will go away and quickly do a lot of investigative work for you, and return a set of results. Then it is over to you to do the detective work. When Warren Buffet was starting out he could only dream of having facilities and tools like this. He had to do his research the old fashioned hard way.

Software tools can only take you so far, unless you are Bill Gates
From the list generated you can then start to look into the business in a lot more detail, read its reports, look at its website, look into its management, and build up as complete a picture as you can about the business until you know it inside out, or at least, feel as though you do. I probably know more about most businesses I invest in than most of the people who work for them.

Remember that past performance is past performance, and you are investing in the future
You should remember that accounts and balance sheets and so on are merely the footsteps of an organisation, and where it has been won't tell you where it is going next. For that you will have to research the business in much greater depth.

In doing the research, investing the time and energy, you are reducing exposure to risk significantly and this knowledge, when applied to the principles we have explored in this book, can help you to identify potential companies that are a value buy and will not only possibly pay you a good dividend, but may also increase in value. That is what is meant by low risk and high reward and it is not rocket science. In fact, it is quite simple.

A firm's income statement may be likened to a bikini – what it reveals is interesting, but what it conceals is vital.

Burton G. Malkiel, *A Random Walk Down Wall Street*

In many cases you should decide not to invest in a business as part of your investigative process. If you are not doing this, that should be a warning sign. I am constantly looking out for investing opportunities and I would estimate that on average no more than five or six businesses meet my criteria in any given year, often fewer, yet I look in detail at hundreds.

What you learn about a business that is not on the balance sheet is as important as what you do, and only through doing so will you gain the necessary understanding to invest wisely and both minimise risk and maximise return.

It's all about great companies

Companies like Coca Cola offer both minimal risk and good returns, and whilst I am not suggesting that you should blindly buy shares in this company, I am suggesting that companies like this can represent an interesting proposition that is worthy of further exploration. You are now in a position to approach investing in the stock market with a knowledge of what you are about, what you aim to achieve that is realistic and takes a long-term view, and some fundamental basics about how to find a business that might be worth your money and which may pay you a nice return in both dividends and an increase in its value.

CHAPTER 32:

Now you own your own business

'The way to get started is to quit talking and begin doing.'

Walt Disney – entrepreneur

BUYING A SHARE IS BUYING A BUSINESS

When you buy a share, you are buying a business. This is literally what happens when you buy shares in a company. The process of buying and selling shares has become so easy via online banking facilities that today's shareholder seems to be forgetting a rather important fact.

DEVELOP AN OWNER MENTALITY

It is not about the process of buying and selling. It is about owning. With owning, comes responsibility. A share is for life, not just for Christmas. Whilst Warren Buffet did not have the advantage of today's time-saving technology when he was starting out, he did have one big advantage in that the old methods of painstakingly researching a business did not alienate you from what you were doing. Sometimes I think that it is almost too easy to buy shares these days. If people were limited to being able to buy only 20 shares in a lifetime, many people would avoid making stupid mistakes. You should pretend that rule applies to you.

Technology, and the internet, have alienated people just as they have also brought people together. Don't get me wrong, I am a huge fan of the internet and regard it as one the greatest developments in recent history, but it does have its drawbacks when it comes to investing, and one of those is the alienating effect it has on detaching the user from the reality of their actions. You are not just pointing and clicking, you are making a commitment when you buy a share and you are agreeing to take ownership of a business and everything that goes with it.

OWNING YOUR OWN BUSINESS IS EASIER THAN YOU IMAGINE

When you buy a share in a business, you become part-owner of that business and whether you are aware of it or not, everyone in that business from the most junior staff to the most senior is now working for you. It is your job to remember this and to exercise your judgement in regard to the quality of the job they are doing.

It is my view that shareholders should not be silent bystanders in a business. You have after all, parted with your hard-earned cash and invested in the enterprise and therefore you are now part-owner of all of its assets, profits and its future. Get involved. It is your money and your business.

If you don't like how the business appears to be run, do something about it. The consistent investor should continue to monitor the performance of all businesses in which they hold a stake, benchmarking it against broadly comparable businesses where appropriate. If someone similar looks as if they are doing much better, you have a right to ask the management of your business why.

BUYING A SHARE IS STARTING A RELATIONSHIP

The process of researching a business and looking into it does not end when and if you make a decision to buy shares in it. That is just the beginning of what should be a long-term relationship. You should continue to monitor and evaluate the performance of the business and continue to learn about it. The more you know about it, the more confident you can be that the decision to keep your money in it is wise. There are, of course, certain rare occasions when you may need to consider selling your interest in a business. Let's look at what those might be.

CHAPTER 33:

There is a time to sell

As a general rule, having gone to all the trouble of identifying a company worth buying and waiting all of the time necessary to buy it at the right time for you, the only time to consider selling it should be when the family has started to look unusually thin and the last candle is nearing its end.

Okay, there are two other scenarios I can think of.

1. Something unforeseeable happens to the company or its management which has a significant impact on its viability as a business to an extent that you would be wise to extract yourself from it and end the relationship. An example of this might be that it turns out that the accountant had been committing fraud and has bankrupted the business for all intents and purposes, or that new legislation will have a severe impact on the ability of the business to continue as a going concern.

Or something like the following scenario which is hopefully more probable:

2. You buy a share in a great company for a fair price. Sure enough over time the share price increases and you feel vindicated that all your hard work has paid dividends. Then the share price really takes off and it goes higher and higher and you start to think crikey you would not have paid that much. Then you start to realise that the price has gone so high only because other people have not been working as hard as you have and have not looked into the business properly at all to work out what a fair price would have been for its shares or what the company is really worth today. You start to realise that the business may be over-valued in your view. So what should you do? Let's look at an example from my own experience concerning the retailer Game Group.

A GOOD EXAMPLE OF KNOWING WHEN TO BUY, AND WHEN TO SELL

Game Group was one of the very early shares that I became interested in. I spent some time researching the business, understood its sector well and had a good sense of where the business was going and the cyclical nature of its particular niche within it. I looked at all of the accounts and knew about as much as I reasonably could. It was also something that I was interested in personally having owned various games consoles for years. It can be a big advantage to the investor to investigate businesses that you have a genuine interest in rather than one that you find dull. It makes the investigative work much more fun. In 2000 you could buy Game Group shares for around 33p a share.

As I have outlined throughout this book, I buy into a business with the general aim of holding the share forever. At least that is the intention and core principle, but you should remember that it is an aspiration or principle, not a law. That said, sometimes under certain circumstances it is prudent to cash in some of your assets when you feel that they have accrued to a level that is not sustainable and then buy back into it again at a lower price, much as I outlined in the Barclays example in the early sections of this book.

If you had bought shares in Game Group in 2000 for around 38p a share you would have seen the price increase to around £1.38 by 2002 and at that point it may have been prudent to sell. Sure enough, the share price a year or so later had dropped to around 38p. By selling at £1.38 a share the investor could have more than quadrupled their money. What is more, the investor could now buy back into Game Group at a price less than 40p and could buy back into it on a ratio of four shares to one in terms of what they had sold at.

In effect the investor could buy a lot more shares in Game Group by merely buying and selling at the right time. But how do you know when to do this?

KNOW THE BUSINESS

The short answer to that question is by knowing the business. Game Group is a games software and console retailer. Games consoles have a lifespan and this tends to be cyclical, typically three to five years. Major game releases are also a key driver in the revenue and profits of Game Group and, by monitoring all of these factors, it is quite possible to make educated projections of how the business will play out. As games consoles near the end of their lives, their sales inevitably drop off, and at that point revenue drops off too. What then happens is usually a time lag between the major console makers like Nintendo, Sony and Microsoft launching their replacement consoles which is the time when Game Group suffers most and, therefore, is the time to buy.

Most people who don't do their homework enough will not really understand the business that Game Group is or the true nature of the niche of games retailing that it is in. Some will, of course, but most will not and will merely follow the herd. So when the price is shooting up, they buy and in many cases are paying over the odds. When the price falls, they panic and sell not realising that in a year or so several new consoles may hit the market and the value and share price of Game Group will once again head north. By the time that most people realise that, they buy back in but buy in at a much higher price, eroding their margin of safety and therefore the likelihood of making any significant gains.

Once again in 2003 it was possible to buy Game Group shares for a price of around 38p. By 2005 they had increased to around 98p. Once again the investor could have trebled their money in a short time. However, at that time Game Group was going from strength to strength. So was it such a good time to sell?

RECOGNISE WHEN YOU GET IT WRONG. IT'S A STRENGTH, NOT A WEAKNESS. ACT QUICKLY AND DECISIVELY TO PUT IT RIGHT

In December 2005 the investor could, at one point, pick up shares in Game Group for around 67p. If they had sold at a previously higher price, once again there was the potential to make money on a gain in the share price over time. If you think you have made a mistake in selling a share too early, recognise the mistake and act on it. Do not try to ignore something if your gut instinct is telling you that you have made an error.

Sure enough the share price of Game Group went up in 2007. I recall reading several share tips around this time advising that Game Group was a 'buy' and sure enough the masses started to fall in once again. The share price went to £1.54, then £1.90 and investors were watching very, very closely for a point at which the share price could be deemed to have peaked. That point arrived in around May 2008 when it hit £2.80. If you had bought at around 67p at the end of 2005 and now in early 2008, barely two years later, your shares were at £2.80 you would have been very pleased indeed.

When you are reading that a share is a 'buy' it is probably beyond the point at which you should consider buying it, as many other people will already be doing so and as Mr Buffet has pointed out, you can't buy what is popular and do well. The time to buy is when others are not, and when the share price of a good or great company is out of fashion, temporarily. It is about thinking independently and rationally and abiding by your core investing principles. That way you may see the opportunity before most other investors do, and that is the mission.

BE HONEST WITH YOURSELF

When I look at the chart for the share price of this business over the last ten years, it would be easy to think that the trends were more predictable then they were. That is not the case. The share price movements of a company like Game Group can be quite cyclical, but remember that the past is no prediction of the future. Remember that what is being advocated here is a rational explanation of why sometimes it is time to sell a share, and buy back in again. It is not a promotion of buying and selling as a desirable activity. This book is not about trading and as carefully explained throughout the two approaches are very different.

Be aware of the political, social and technological changes taking place that may impact on a business like Game Group. I have some reservations about suggesting that the future behaviour of the price of a business like Game Group will follow previous cyclical trends not least because of changes that are taking place in regard to technology. Mobile technology and downloads will inevitably impact on the traditional business model of Game Group and I do not currently see a clear business strategy that will position the business favourably in this new environment.

However, because it has been such a relatively predictable share to watch over time in the past, I wanted to use it as an illustration of how share price movements in a particular business can be expected. I will make a small prediction on where it might go next, just for fun.

I DON'T OFFER PREDICTIONS, BUT . . .

I have commented previously that nobody should make predictions about share prices for you and that you should form your own opinion, and I will stick to that. I am not in the business of advising anyone on what to buy or what to sell, rather I am keen to provide signposts to learning an approach and taking a range of measures that will help you to achieve your financial aims. That said, I feel that it is appropriate to comment a little on the Game Group example beyond the time of writing this book if only to enable the reader to form a view of the credibility of my comments on this example.

At the time of writing, the share price of Game Group is £1.76. Nobody can predict what its price will be next week, next month or the month after that. However, I will watch this business as it follows what I expect to be a pattern that is peculiar to the games console and software business. In the next year or two, all of the main manufacturers will start to announce their development plans for their next machines and in doing so, will provide a broad outline of their release dates. No manufacturer will want to be a late entrant in this market as Sony have learnt to their significant cost with the ill-fated PS3 which was damaged by being late into the market and over-priced when it did eventually make its entrance. It damaged the Playstation brand significantly and allowed the outsiders to capture their market share. They will be looking to get that back.

The point is that in the year before most of these machines are released, the share price of Game Group is likely to be a lot lower than it would otherwise be. This is primarily because their revenue will be waning as their customers wait for the release of the new machines following which revenues and the value of the business in theory go up, all things remaining equal (which they might not).

Just before that happens is the time most likely to get Game Group shares at a bargain price and capitalise on it. Of course, it may not happen that way next time around, but I am using the Game Group share price fluctuation as an example of how you might use an on-going relationship with a particular business to your advantage. I think Game Group shares are likely to be cheap at some point in the medium-term future and my estimation would be that this point will be broadly within a year of when the next generation of games consoles is released. Whilst I have no idea when that will be, I expect the patterns of the past will in all probability happen again for this business, due to its cyclical nature combined with the volume of traders and speculators who have not researched and understood their share-buying behaviour adequately. I may of course be totally wrong about this but it is worth keeping an eye on this example.

This is your unfair advantage. Do your work, study a business, and use the ignorance and laziness of others to your advantage where you can. It is not about being right 100% of the time. Even Warren Buffet can't achieve that. It is about being right more often than being wrong, and when you are right, how right you are, and when you are wrong, how wrong you are.

CHAPTER 34:

The craft of consistent investing

'Education consists mainly of what we have unlearned.'

Mark Twain – American author

LEARNING DOESN'T STOP, IT JUST GETS BETTER

Whilst the consistent investor should always strive to adhere to a set of investment principles suited to his or her personality and investment objectives, it is a constant learning process. The actual skills that will determine your relative success in investing will be determined as much by your vision and creativity as they will by your ability to read financial statements. It is a constant learning process. What worked for you once may not work for you again. Warren Buffet was always acutely aware of this and nearly walked away from investing on several occasions when he felt that he no longer understood the landscape he found himself in.

'Anyone who stops learning is old, whether at twenty or eighty.'

Henry Ford – founder of the Ford Motor Company

Investing is a craft. No craft can have an out-of-the-box solution. This is why the world of 'investment strategies' and one-size-fits-all solutions on how to 'play' the stock market will never work and are most unhelpful to the person starting out on their investment career. They may seem appealing and 'easy' but that is a seductive illusion. To achieve your ambitions, it is inevitable that you will have to put in some hard work.

The stock market is but a trading mechanism. It will tell you the price of something, not its value. Traders and speculators will therefore often cause considerable volatility in the share price movements of a business, but only in understanding what you deem to be the real value of the business will you be able to estimate what a reasonable price for that business is, and whether it is worth buying in the first place at all.

> '*I conceive that the great part of the miseries of mankind are brought upon them by false estimates they have made of the value of things.*'
>
> Benjamin Franklin, 1706–1790 – American politician, inventor and scientist

YOU CAN DO IT

With the right approach, in time you should learn to recognise businesses that may be under-valued and which may be rising stars of the future. When Vincent van Gogh started painting, he hoped that one day his paintings would be recognised as being worth more than the value of the paint and the canvas that they were on. I would imagine that most investors with a time machine would like to go back and meet Mr van Gogh at that point, and probably buy as many of his paintings as were available.

> '*It's what you learn after you know it all that counts.*'
>
> Attributed to Harry S. Truman – 33rd President of the US

Like any craft, investing will take time and skill and commitment, but starts with a simple interest, or desire, to learn and to always guard against the intoxicating effects of your success, or the over-blown impacts of a failure. A road may have many twists and turns and bumps, but if you are on the right road, you will eventually reach your destination. Turning back at the first bump will achieve nothing.

LEARNING FROM THE MASTERS

A key part of the learning process is to target those whom you hold in high regard and learn from them. I have studied Warren Buffet in great detail, not because I think I can emulate his approach and nor should I try to anyway, but simply because he has mastered his particular craft.

Masters play a game where the rules are known to everyone, but then apply them in a way that nobody else did. Much of what Buffet has achieved and done was not brilliant in itself,

'A single conversation with a wise man is better than ten years of study.'

Chinese Proverb

but what separated him from other money managers was the way in which he did not deviate from his own approach even in the face of much adversity. Warren Buffet never followed the fashions and fads of investing, rather periodically throughout his life they caught up with him at various points.

That is the challenge for the investor. Learn the rules and guiding principles, some of which have been alluded to in this book, and then apply them in a way that makes sense to you. If you like higher risk investments, do your research well, follow the guidance you have learned from reading as much as you can in screening businesses that meet your criteria and objectives, then that may well work for you. Equally, others may take a more cautious approach.

What I have tried to convey is that nothing is as simple as it may first appear but at the same time, often it is not as complicated either. The way forward is often a combination of what might seem like contradictory factors, such as low risk and high reward, and I have attempted to show what is meant by this approach. Investing is a constantly challenging and rewarding process, but remember that you will never have mastered the market. You will always remain its servant, albeit one that hopefully does very well indeed.

CHAPTER 35:
Some additional signposts

'The four most expensive words in the English language are, "This time it's different".'

Sir John Templeton – investor

STICK TO WHAT WORKS

Although the world is constantly changing, some things remain the same. Sticking to the speed limit when driving was a good idea 50 years ago, and it remains so today. Not running with a pair of scissors has always been good advice. Not sticking metal objects in the toaster when it is switched on has been good advice for as long as we have had toasters, and, as far as I can see, it will remain so. Yet every generation seems to have to learn its lessons the hard way. I was recently in a cemetery where there was a grave of a young boy who died within several days of his 19th birthday. I was curious as to what had happened and a little investigation revealed that he was killed in a road traffic accident caused by excessive speed.

You might be thinking what on earth has this got to do with investing in the stock market? Well, today someone, somewhere will spend more money than they can afford buying shares in a business that is the latest 'emerging opportunity' and a chance to make 'big gains' and they will learn their lesson the hard way in the same way as the boy in the graveyard, although admittedly they will pay only a financial price. Yet this can all be largely avoided.

THE PAST WON'T PREDICT THE FUTURE, BUT IT CAN MAKE INFORMED SUGGESTIONS ABOUT IT

I have never been a fan of history. My history teacher at school was an eccentric man who looked two days older than God and had a remarkable resemblance to Slartibartfast from the *Hitchhiker's Guide to the Galaxy* by Douglas Adams. That probably didn't help. The reason I never really valued history when I was younger was because I could not understand its relevance to today. The past after all, is no prediction of the future.

That said, sometimes it can provide you with signposts to the direction things are moving in if you are looking hard enough to spot them. You may have had the privilege of listening to an older person who says that they have seen it all before. Indeed, they probably have, and you would be well advised to listen to the wise, should you ever be presented with the opportunity.

Should you not find yourself lucky enough to know someone who manages a nursing home for successful former Wall Street money managers, you can turn to any number of great books worth investigating and I will make a few suggestions here. Many of the best books and much of the wisdom you will ever gain access to was written down some time ago, or practised by people who may now be in the twilight of their days. Read everything you can about such people. You never know, you might learn something.

These are my suggestions for some further reading. These suggestions were based upon their ability to stand the test of time. Many investing fashions come and go, but some of the principles consistently practised by some of the greatest money managers that have ever lived are still as relevant today. So here goes, just a few recommendations for further reading amongst a large pool of knowledge that exists out there.

- *The Intelligent Investor* by Benjamin Graham (HarperCollins, 2003).
- *The Snowball: Warren Buffet and the Business of Life* by Alice Schroeder (Bloomsbury Publishing, 2009).
- *The Essays of Warren Buffet: Lessons for Investors and Managers* by L.A. Cunningham (Wiley and Sons, 2009).
- *One Up on Wall Street* by Peter Lynch with John Rothchild (Simon and Schuster, 2000).

Happy reading.

CHAPTER 36:

Guiding principles for the consistent investor

'I view my life in a way . . . I'll explain it to you, OK? The greatest thing about tomorrow is, I will be better than I am today. And that's how I look at my life. I will be better as a golfer, I will be better as a person, I will be better as a father, I will be a better husband, I will be better as a friend. That's the beauty of tomorrow. There is no such thing as a setback. The lessons I learn today I will apply tomorrow, and I will be better.'

Tiger Woods – sportsman

So what did we learn on this short journey?

Let's summarise a few of the key messages.

KNOW YOURSELF

Before investing, take time to understand your goals and realistic aspirations, and consider how you will behave under pressure.

BE CONSISTENT

Formulate an approach that you aspire to apply consistently. Do not follow the crowd unless there is a very good reason to do so. Following the crowd out of a building that is on fire is generally a good idea. Following a lemming off a cliff is not.

UNDERSTAND THE BUSINESS

Buying something you don't understand is stupid and you will lose money. You don't need to understand how to make a missile to invest in a defence company, but you do need to understand something about the sector as well as who is running the business, where it is going, who its customers are, whether it is making money and what you think a reasonable price for it is, etc.

TIME IS YOUR ALLY AND ONE OF THE GREATEST INVESTING TOOLS. USE IT

Learn to be patient. It is a skill that will serve you well. Having found a business that you love, applying patience may mean waiting, not until the coming Friday to buy the share, but waiting until a Friday four years from now. Seriously. If you can apply that kind of patience in your investing, your returns are likely to be far higher than wading into investing in a business before you have built a comfortable margin of safety into the price. The rewards from applying patience will far exceed any 'buy it now' mentality.

APPRECIATE RISK

Understand and appreciate how to manage your exposure to risk in all of its guises. Build a margin of safety into most of your measures when looking to invest in a business and always strive to buy at below the real intrinsic value of the company.

BUY INTO GREAT BUSINESSES THAT YOU LOVE

Buy great businesses at fair prices. Even better, cheap prices. During the financial crisis that hit the world in 2008, I bought stocks in carefully screened financial institutions at a time when most would not have touched them. Most people were actually getting out of shares completely at that time. I bought into Barclays, HSBC, Santander and Wells Fargo. In less than one year, the share prices of those companies have dramatically increased and whilst they may go down and then go back up and then go down in the coming months and years, buying a solid business is more important than buying weaker businesses for what you perceive to be a bargain price. Always buy quality. Always consider what defence the business has against changing fortunes. Always consider what its competitive advantage is, and how easily that might be eroded.

LOOK FOR GROWTH

Invest in growing businesses. If a business is not growing you would have to have a very good reason indeed to buy into it if you consider yourself to be an investor and not a speculator. The profit should be growing year on year, as should the turnover.

LOOK FOR DIVIDENDS THAT ARE GOOD, BUT NOT EXCESSIVE

Look for companies that have both the potential for growth in their share price but also which pay dividends. Where dividends are concerned, anything over 5% in terms of a dividend yield and that also meets all of the other criteria that you are looking for, is good. Buying a share of a great company at a fair price and which pays a good dividend provides you with a margin of safety in getting it wrong. Should the share price drop a little, you should hopefully still be compensated somewhat by the dividend.

AVOID DEBT

As in your own life, avoid debt where possible. A business with a high level of debt will always be vulnerable to changing financial fortunes and wider unforeseen events. A net gearing ratio of less than 35% is generally desirable. Very strong and large companies can service higher levels of debt without compromising their sustainability but smaller enterprises that have over 35% net gearing are more vulnerable and you should always exercise caution here.

LOOK FOR QUALITY MANAGEMENT

Look into the people running a business that you are considering investing in. Consider how much they pay themselves in relation to the performance of the business and take note of their full benefits package as detailed in the financial statements. Excessive pay is a dangerous sign, and I have often seen this combined with a company that is slowly dying. Self-serving directors and managers will kill off a half decent company over time. You should monitor this closely. If the people running the business appear to be doing so in their interests at the expense of their shareholders, you should seriously consider whether to put your money into their pockets.

You should also consider how responsibly the management behave in their dealings with the business, and how frank they appear through what they write in the various company reports. If something is written in a style that seems ambiguous and confusing, there is often a reason, and it should set your alarm bells ringing. There is no reason at all why any public reports should be confusing or overly technical. Remember that. Pay equal attention to what a management team actually does and say they will do. Often too much focus is on the words, rather than actions and results. A leadership whose achievements are mostly in the future should give you great concern.

DIVERSIFY, INTELLIGENTLY

Practise selective diversification. This does not mean randomly buying companies in different sectors in the belief that it will somehow reduce your risk. Rather, carefully research and select a range of different types of businesses such as large and small, UK and overseas, different industry sectors and so on, taking the time to fully understand each business, how it is run, and why you would want to own it. Owning shares in five different companies that are all in the defence sector as the world heads through a recession would not be wise diversification.

AVOID FADS AND MARKETING SPIN

Avoid investment fads (recent examples being green companies such as renewable energy companies etc.). Often it is the companies which are offering nothing new which will deliver the best returns. Be especially wary of those keen to share their advice with you, and whilst it is always worth reading share tips and considering the widest range of different views that you can, you should guard against attaching too much significance to them. Your own research, and the quality of it, is what really counts.

LEARN FROM PEOPLE YOU ADMIRE

Following this point, be especially wary of whose advice you value. Look at the people who have been most successful at what they do and consider and reflect on this. Warren Buffet is a great example as he is an engaging character to read about, but there are many others such as George Soros or Jim Rogers who have made a lot of money in their own way.

Do not think for a moment that you can imitate what they did; you will only become disenchanted, as you will if you compare yourself to others in life in general. That is not the point at all. Rather, learn from how they thought about their investing behaviour, and how it worked for them at that time in a way that was relevant to that moment. Even for the most successful, the successes of the past become increasingly harder to maintain over time. Warren Buffet himself is predicting much slower growth for his investment vehicle Berkshire Hathaway in the future, largely due to its size but also because we are probably entering a period in world history where economic growth will be less than historical levels. Accept that and be realistic about what you are setting out to achieve.

Understand that by doing your research well, boring as it may be, you will reduce risk at the same time as increasing your potential reward. 'Low risk and high reward' is your investment mantra.

DEVELOP AN OWNER MENTALITY

When you buy a share in a business you become part-owner of that business. You should appreciate that with ownership comes a responsibility. If you do not take that responsibility seriously, you may increase the odds of you losing money. Take it seriously and get involved in the business, and you will be more likely to understand the life of the business, where it is going, how it is being run, and how profitable it is likely to be.

Passive investing works only if you buy into large established investment trusts or a massive business like Coca Cola or Tesco. However, even then I would argue that no investment should be passive. Owning a company should be an involving and interactive process. Keep on top of the business, and you should use your online share-dealing facility to consistently monitor your investments by receiving news items and any other relevant notification. I have set up mine to alert me to any significant changes in the price of my investments by a specific margin. I rarely get these alerts since I have set them up to notify me only if something is going very badly wrong, and to date, that is a rare occurrence in ten years.

SEE THE VALUE, NOT THE PRICE

No matter how much you want to buy a share in a business, do not pay over the odds for it. There is a number of ways of working out a good price for a share, whether you average the price of it over ten years or so, or build future facing ratios into it to give an idea of value or any other of a number of increasingly-scientific methods doesn't really matter. The point is that you need to be as confident as you can be that you are getting the share for a good price and one that is likely to increase. In order to know whether that is likely to happen or not, you will need to have done your research properly.

SOMETIMES YOU WILL NEED TO SELL. THIS SHOULD BE EXCEPTIONAL

Although I have consistently emphasised that you should buy a share only in a business that you would want to own indefinitely, there is sometimes a reason to sell. If a share price has risen spectacularly and is well above what you deem to be the intrinsic value of it, you would be foolish not to sell most of your shares in it. I say most, because when I do this, I always retain an interest in the business. That way if I am wrong and the share price continues to soar, then I still benefit. If I am right and the share price is about to plummet, I realise a significant profit which I can then choose to re-invest in the same business, in many cases at a fraction of the recent cost. This strategy works only where the business in question is a great one but which is being afflicted by a temporary storm leading to irrational behaviour in the market.

Sell high, wait, then buy back in at a low price and wait for it to repeat. It is a cycle. Judging when to buy in and when to cash in will be your critical success factors here. Remember, this type of behaviour is exceptional, not the norm. You should guard against too much trading. If you feel the need to do this, then you are probably not picking your shares selectively enough and are unlikely to be following a consistent investment approach. I merely highlight this message because, despite the best efforts of the consistent investor, sometimes there is indeed a time to sell.

NURTURE A PASSION FOR LEARNING

Investing is a craft. Nobody can claim to have it sussed or have a formula or system that works universally. You will continue to learn for as long as you are engaged in it. That applies as much to the great Warren Buffet as it does to anyone on the street, although Warren probably has a lot less left to learn than most.

It is the constant learning process that makes investing so rewarding. Whilst increasing your wealth can bring its own rewards, it is the lessons and discoveries that you learn along the way that will perhaps provide you with the greatest development. I would recommend you start by looking at the best in the world, and hope that some of it rubs off on you.

'If I have seen farther than others, it is because I was standing on the shoulder of giants.'

Isaac Newton – English physicist

Index

HOW TO MAKE MONEY FROM PROPERTY

Easy to read, authentic and up to date advice on investing in property

AJAY AHUJA

There are a surprising number of ways that you can make money from property. This book will not only explain those ways but will help you decide which method is right for you based on your personal profile and attitude to risk. Ajay Ahuja has been in property for 13 years. His property sourcing business actually grew by 400% during the credit crunch whilst all his other competitors fell by the wayside. He has been involved with pretty much every type of property business there is and he shares his wisdom – and his passion - in this easy to read and informative book.

ISBN 978-1-84528-411-4

HOW TO INVEST IN THE UK PROPERTY MARKET

GERRY FITZGERALD

'Not only covers all the information you need about the nuts and bolts of investing in property but offers real gems of inside information.' The Oxford Times, Lettings

ISBN 978-1-84528-244-8

THE BEGINNER'S GUIDE TO PROPERTY INVESTMENT

TONY BOOTH

'This book draws on Tony's extensive knowledge and experience in the property industry and covers issues from buying a property at auction to buy-to-let, from self-building to finding the right mortgage. His advice should help ensure a sound investment.' – In the Sticks

ISBN 978-1-85703-961-0

HOW TO BE A PROPERTY MILLIONAIRE
ANNIE HULLEY

'A must-read book. Annie Hulley's experiences are real and the book systematically goes through the process of buying, selling, letting and investing in property in the UK and abroad.' – The Overseas Property Professional

ISBN 978-1-85703-857-6

THE BUY TO LET MANUAL
TONY BOOTH

'An excellent piece of work that clearly and concisely encapsulates the fundamental issues.' *Philip R Gibbs, Life President of the Residential Landlords Association*

ISBN 978-1-84528-252-3

THE LANDLORD'S SURVIVAL GUIDE
LESLEY HENDERSON

'The book covers a range of topics. It's a must-have for anyone considering a buy-to-let investment.' HotProperty

ISBN 978-1-84528-224-0

THE NEW LANDLORD'S GUIDE TO LETTING
MOIRA STEWART

'. . . a comprehensive guide . . . gives you the information that you need to manage a small portfolio of rented properties.' – Investors Chronicle

ISBN 978-1-84528-179-3

How To Books are available through all good bookshops, or you can order direct from us through Grantham Book Services.

Tel: +44 (0)1476 541080
Fax: +44 (0)1476 541061
Email: orders@gbs.tbs-ltd.co.uk

Or via our website

www.howtobooks.co.uk

To order via any of these methods please quote the title(s) of the book(s) and your credit card number together with its expiry date.

For further information about our books and catalogue, please contact:

How To Books
Spring Hill House
Spring Hill Road
Begbroke
Oxford
OX5 1RX

Visit our web site at

www.howtobooks.co.uk

Or you can contact us by email at info@howtobooks.co.uk